My Cousin Rachel

A Play

Adapted by
DIANA MORGAN

from the novel by
DAPHNE DU MAURIER

SAMUEL   FRENCH

LONDON
NEW YORK   TORONTO   SYDNEY   HOLLYWOOD

FOR AMATEUR PRODUCTION ENQUIRIES

UNITED KINGDOM AND WORLD
EXCLUDING NORTH AMERICA
plays@SamuelFrench-London.co.uk
020 7255 4302/01

Each title is subject to availability from Samuel French,
depending upon country of performance.

CHARACTERS

Rachel Ashley
Philip Ashley
Nicholas Kendall
Louise Kendall
Antonio Rainaldi
Seecombe
James

The action takes place at Barton Hall

Time—mid-nineteenth century

PRODUCTION NOTE

The Curtain should not be dropped between the scenes. Lapses of time should be denoted by the fading down and fading up of Lights

ACT I

The Hall at Barton. Night

This is the Great Hall of a large Cornish Manor House. At the back are a big window and a door leading to the drive and the garden. To one side a staircase leads to a gallery, and on the opposite side is a door to the servants' quarters. Below the staircase is a door leading to the dining-room

It is dark. Candles flicker. There is a distant rumble of thunder

Seecombe, the elderly, shabby steward enters from the servants' quarters, carrying a candle in a jam pot. He is followed by James pulling on a jerkin. Seecombe waves the boy out to the front door and puts down the jam pot. A horse is heard neighing. James returns, carrying a valise

James Do I put it in Master Philip's room?
Seecombe No, put it in Mr Ashley's old room.

As James goes to the stairs, half-followed by Seecombe, Philip Ashley enters. He is young, sensitive looking, obviously very exhausted. He wears a coat with a cape and carries a small travelling-case. Seecombe takes the case and hands it to James

See that the fire's still going. Go on, lad!

James goes upstairs

Philip I beg that no-one makes a fuss, Seecombe.
Seecombe We've all been so worried, Mr Philip. It's been such a time. And we were afraid you might take the fever like poor Mr Ashley.
Philip I'm not ill, Seecombe. Only very tired. It's a long journey from Florence.
Seecombe Best part of three weeks.
Philip Yes. Well, I'm for bed. We'll talk in the morning.
Seecombe I took the liberty of informing Mr Kendall of your return, sir. I sent James over to Pelyn when I got your letter.
Philip Thank you.
Seecombe And I also took the liberty of making up the bed in poor Mr Ashley's room.
Philip Ambrose's room. (*Pause*) Yes, that will do very well.

James comes downstairs

Seecombe You must be hungry, sir. I'll send up a tray.
Philip No nothing to eat—just a hot brandy and lemon. Good night.

*Seecombe gives Philip the candle and he goes slowly upstairs, opens the
door, and when he shuts it the stage is in darkness*

There is a distant rumble of thunder and the wind rises

The Lights fade

SCENE 2

The same. The next morning

*Sunshine streaming through the great window reveals the shabby interior—
dust and cobwebs everywhere. The door-bell clangs. Silence. It clangs again*

*Seecombe enters and crosses towards the door and pulls it open. Louise
Kendall enters. She is a pretty girl of about eighteen, hoydenish, wearing a
riding-habit. She is followed by Nicholas Kendall, her father, an attractive
man in his fifties. He wears a black arm-band and carries a leather case*

Louise (*radiantly*) Seecombe, where is he?
Seecombe Mr Philip came late and went straight to his bed, Miss Louise.
  He was worn out. Foreign parts is a long way off as I said—and they
  don't come no foreigner than Italy—on account of the Italians no doubt.
  I'll tell him you're here, Miss.
Louise Hurry, Seecombe, hurry ...!
Kendall Don't be so impatient, Louise.

Seecombe goes off upstairs and disappears

Louise (*removing her gloves*) I hope he won't be long—I'm dying to hear ...
Kendall Louise ...!
Louise Father?
Kendall You're a sensible girl, Louise. I beg you to be so now ...
Louise Oh, Father ...!
Kendall Be careful what you say to Philip. Ambrose Ashley was everything
  to Philip—the only family he has ever known. He was much more than a
  cousin to him—he was father, mother, brother, friend. Ambrose's death
  is a sad thing for all of us—but it is a tragedy for Philip. He may want to
  talk about it—on the other hand he may not. I beg that you do not rush
  him. He'll need time to find himself, to put the past eighteen months
  behind him and realize that he is now master of Barton.

Seecombe comes downstairs

Seecombe Mr Philip will be with you presently.
Kendall Thank you.
Seecombe Some refreshment, sir?
Kendall Not at the moment Seecombe.
Seecombe Miss Louise?

Louise shakes her head

  Seecombe exits

Louise How strange it is. Ambrose dead and Philip ... How strange everything is—Ambrose marrying like that was strange.

Kendall Yes.

Louise Meeting this Cousin Rachel in Florence and marrying her after a few weeks. Oh, I do wonder what she's like!

Kendall Now, Louise!

Louise I expect she's very fascinating.

Kendall Why?

Louise Well she caught an old bachelor like Ambrose—she must be fascinating.

Kendall Ambrose wasn't old. My age.

Louise Well you're hardly a chicken, Father. Never mind, Mary Pascoe said you must have been very fascinating—once.

Kendall snorts

Philip runs down the staircase and greets them

Philip Louise. Uncle Nick.

Kendall Good to see you, Philip. What sort of a journey did you have?

Philip It was very rough in the Bay. Louise, I brought you this. (*He hands her a small package*)

Louise (*delightedly*) Oh Phil! (*She starts to open it*)

Kendall You spoil her.

Philip So do you. By the way did Seecombe offer you any refreshment?

Kendall Yes. But we dined early thank you.

Louise (*displaying a necklace*) Oh Phil—it's beautiful! How clever of you. I love amber. Did you know?

Philip As a matter of fact I asked the man in the shop what a young lady would like. I'm not very good at that sort of thing.

Louise (*disappointedly*) I see.

Short pause

Philip Well Uncle Nick, you'll be wanting to hear my news.

Kendall Yes.

Philip It's difficult to know where to begin.

Kendall You arrived in Florence ...

Philip Yes, and went straight to the villa. When I got there the butler told me that Ambrose had been dead for three weeks.

Louise It must have been a dreadful shock. Poor Philip.

Philip Yes.

Kendall What then?

Philip I asked for Mrs Ashley.

Kendall Yes?

Philip I was told that she had left Florence immediately after the funeral, taking all Ambrose's possessions with her.

Louise So you didn't see her?

Philip No.

Louise Oh, I *am* disappointed. Ever since Ambrose wrote and said he'd

married his Cousin Rachel, I've longed to know what she was like. I was
just saying to Father that I was sure she must be very fascinating or
Ambrose would never have married her, wasn't I, Father?

Kendall Stop chattering, Louise. Go on, Philip.

Philip I went to see her man of business, Signor Rainaldi. Ambrose had
mentioned him in his letters. I didn't like him. In fact I detested him.

Kendall What was wrong with him?

Philip I can rely on you, Uncle Nick, and you, Louise, can't I?

Kendall I've been your guardian for twenty-four years, Philip.

Philip Did you wonder why I rushed out to Italy so suddenly?

Kendall Ambrose was ill.

Philip takes a letter from his pocket and hands it to Kendall

Philip Read that.

Kendall begins to read it

Aloud. I want Louise to hear.

Kendall (*reading*) ". . . There is no-one I can trust. She watches me con-
tinually. Sometimes I think that money is the only way to her heart. I
don't trust Rainaldi, nor the doctor he recommended to me. I shall try
to smuggle this letter out of the house. I will beat them yet . . . Why
must she lie to me all the time? . . . Ambrose." Poor Ambrose. Poor
fellow. Just like his father.

Philip What do you mean?

Kendall His father died of brain fever, too. In his last days he turned
against everyone he loved, particularly his wife.

Philip Ambrose's marriage was a great shock.

Kendall I know. But given time it might have proved a blessing.

Philip A blessing?

Kendall Yes. This house needed a woman. The monastic life you lived
here was unnatural.

Philip We were happy.

Kendall You thought you were happy. Go on.

Philip Then Ambrose gets ill and I get that letter. I go to Italy, find he has
died very suddenly, find that his wife has disappeared, get no satisfaction
out of this Rainaldi fellow, come back yesterday to find a last letter from
Ambrose has arrived during my absence. (*He takes out another letter*)
It's very short—I'll read it to you. "Come quickly . . . she has done for
me . . . Rachel, my torment . . ."

Kendall Well?

Philip Don't you understand? Don't you see what I am implying?

Kendall Certainly. You are implying that there is something—something
not . . . Damn it all, Philip, you are implying that Mrs Ashley had
something to do with her husband's death.

Philip Yes.

Kendall You'd better be careful, my boy. If you spread a rumour like
this—and it got to her ears . . .

Philip I wish it to get to her ears.

Louise Philip!

Kendall You're talking like a madman, Philip. Now, you listen to me. Ambrose, who had not been well, gets a bad attack of Roman fever. It goes to his brain exactly as it did to his father's. He died in Rome when Ambrose was still a child. You have no evidence, no evidence whatever against Mrs Ashley. She had nothing to gain from her husband's death—and everything to lose. I am amazed that we have not heard of any new will drawn up in her favour. As things stand you get everything and she gets nothing. So you be careful, Philip.

Philip Just wait until I find out where she is—that's all.

Kendall *I* can tell you where she is.

Philip *You* can?

Kendall She's in Plymouth. I had a letter from her this morning—she has brought all Ambrose's possessions with her. I am going to ask her to stay with Louise and me while she is in England. She is the widow of my oldest friend.

Louise Oh, Father! How fascinating . . .

Philip In Plymouth . . .

Kendall She has also brought with her a great number of plants and seeds which she and Ambrose had collected. It was their love of gardening that first brought them together.

Philip (*slowly*) The villa had a beautiful garden.

Louise Then I shall see her at last! Oh—I do wonder what she's like.

Kendall I shall write to her tonight conveying the invitation.

Philip No. She is Ambrose's widow. She must come here.

Kendall After what you've just been saying?

Philip It would look very strange if she stayed elsewhere.

Kendall Agreed. But if you are going to accuse her . . .

Philip (*interrupting*) I am not going to accuse her.

Kendall A few moments ago . . .

Philip (*interrupting*) Tell her that Philip Ashley is a plain man and that Barton is a plain man's home—but that she is welcome.

Kendall Can I trust you, Philip, to behave properly towards the poor woman?

Philip I give you my word, Uncle Nick.

Kendall Very well. Now I must go and see old Tamblyn. There's been some trouble with his lease. Louise?

Louise I think I'll stay for a bit, Father. Perhaps Philip will see me home.

Philip Of course.

Kendall makes for the main door. He pauses there

Kendall Philip . . .

Philip It's all right, Uncle Nick.

Kendall goes out

Louise Oh, Phil—isn't it fascinating? We shall see her at last. I'm so excited. What do you think she looks like?

Philip Like a snake.

Louise I don't. I see her tall and stately—a real Roman matron. How old is she?

Philip I've no idea. She has rheumatism—I know that—that's why she and Ambrose didn't come back last winter.

Louise Oh, then she must be quite old. Well on in her thirties. Little and bent and going grey. Phil . . .

Philip Yes.

Louise Do you—do you really think there was something—well, odd about Ambrose's death?

Philip Yes.

Louise But what can you do about it?

Philip I can watch her. I shall know.

Louise If she is—what you think—won't you be a bit frightened?

Philip Frightened? Of a woman?

Louise You don't know any women.

Philip I know you.

Louise I'm only a girl.

Philip I am not in the least frightened of my Cousin Rachel. She should be frightened of *me*.

Louise bursts out laughing

Louise Philip, really!

Philip I mean it.

Louise Of all the pompous . . .

Philip I mean it.

Louise stops laughing abruptly

Louise How peculiar . . .

Philip What is?

Louise To see you looking like that. Like a stranger.

Philip Rubbish.

Louise Do you remember that old gypsy we met at Penhallow Fair?

Philip Vaguely. Why?

Louise She said you were like a sunlit pool—but only on the surface.

Philip What *are* you talking about?

Louise I've known you all my life.

Philip What of it?

Louise For a moment you were a stranger. I think I'd better be going.

Philip As you wish.

There is a pause as Louise picks up her riding-crop

Louise I suppose you'll be going in to Plymouth to meet Mrs Ashley.

Philip No.

Louise But, Philip . . .

Philip I shall send the carriage.

Louise But, Philip, you must go.

Philip Why?

Louise She is your guest—Ambrose's widow.

Philip I am far too busy to waste time going to Plymouth. I shall leave instructions with the servants.
Louise But it's such bad manners.
Philip Don't try to teach me how to behave, Louise.
Louise Why not? Someone should teach you common courtesy.
Philip Someone should teach you to mind your own business.

They stand glaring at each other

Louise breaks away and runs out. Seecombe enters

Seecombe, Mrs Ashley is in England and will be coming to stay here.
Seecombe (*open-mouthed*) Mr Ambrose's wife?
Philip Mr Ashley's widow.
Seecombe Coming here?
Philip Yes. You'd better get the Pink Room ready.
Seecombe The floorboards have gone, sir.
Philip The room over the library then.
Seecombe It's got the woodworm.
Philip Lady Mary's Chamber.
Seecombe She walks most nights.
Philip Damn it, Seecombe, what's wrong with the Oak Room?
Seecombe Mice, Mr Philip.
Philip Get out Seecombe and if a room isn't ready by the time she comes I'll—I'll have you beaten with rods.
Seecombe Very good, sir. Will that be all, sir?
Philip More than enough! (*He roars*) Out, out!

Seecombe goes

Philip shakes himself as if trying to clear his head from bewilderment

Mrs Ashley ... Coming here ...

The Lights fade

SCENE 3

The same. A few days later. Evening

Seecombe is arranging flowers in a silver rose-bowl. Philip enters by the main door

Philip What on earth are you doing, Seecombe?
Seecombe Ladies like flowers in a room, Mr Philip.
Philip She's come?
Seecombe Madam arrived at four o'clock. She said she would dine in her room. James took her up a tray. At what hour will you dine, sir?
Philip I dined in Bodmin. That will be all, Seecombe.
Seecombe Very good, Mr Philip. Madam asked to be informed when you arrived.
Philip Well, inform her then.

Seecombe inclines his head, goes up the stairs and knocks at a door

Seecombe Mr Philip has returned, madam.
Rachel (*off*) Thank you, Seecombe.

Seecombe comes down the stairs and exits through the servants' door

Philip moves restlessly about, clenching and unclenching his hands

The door upstairs opens and Rachel emerges, carrying a candle which illuminates her face. She is a beautiful woman in her early thirties, tall and slender. She is dressed exquisitely in black. She comes slowly downstairs. At the foot of the stairs, she pauses and looks across at Philip

Ambrose . . . You are so like . . .

Philip moves forward

Philip Welcome to Barton, Cousin Rachel.
Rachel Thank you.
Philip I regret I was not at home to welcome you.
Rachel You are a busy man. Ambrose told me how hard you worked. I quite understand.
Philip I hope the servants have made you quite comfortable.
Rachel Very comfortable, thank you. (*Pause. She sits down in the armchair*) You must be wondering why I came to England. It was on your account—and Ambrose's.
Philip Indeed?
Rachel He thought the world of you. "My Philip"—he would say. I know he would like you to have his personal possessions and he would have wanted the plants and shrubs we had so lovingly collected to find their proper home.
Philip He loved the garden.
Rachel He loved everything about Barton. He used to talk about it by the hour. Bore Town and Borden's Meadow, Kemp Close and Beef Park, Kilmore and Beacon Field, the Twenty Acres and the West Hills.
Philip (*surprised*) You seem to know the names of all the Barton lands.
Rachel He was so looking forward to showing them to me. We would sit in the courtyard at the villa, drinking our tisane, and instead of the sunshine I would see the grey seas breaking over Star Point and hear the seagulls crying.
Philip This is your first visit to England?
Rachel Yes. My first husband, Count Sangaletti used to promise to bring me here for a visit, but he was killed in an accident. From what I have seen of the countryside, Cornwall is very lovely. Very wild and exciting.
Philip (*abruptly*) You know I came to Florence?
Rachel Yes. Signor Rainaldi wrote and told me. It must have been terrible for you. I wish I had known you were coming.
Philip Ambrose wrote and begged me.
Rachel I know he was very anxious to see you.
Philip Did he know how ill he was?
Rachel Possibly. But he was homesick—and you represented home to him.
Philip He died very suddenly.

Rachel He had seemed better, less—less strange.
Philip Strange?
Rachel When he first became ill, nothing I, or the doctors, could do would satisfy him. It was as if we had become his enemies.
Philip Indeed?
Rachel It is often so. Pressure on the brain, the doctors told me. Then he suddenly seemed better—more like the Ambrose I knew and loved. We began to make plans. And then one evening . . .
Philip Yes?
Rachel I was sitting by his bed. He seemed asleep. Then he—he opened his eyes and said: "Rachel" and fell back on the pillows . . . We had only been married eighteen months.

Pause

Philip (*awkwardly*) May I get you a glass of wine?
Rachel Thank you no. Presently Seecombe will bring me some hot water and I will make the tisane that Ambrose and I loved. I asked him . . . Oh, I do hope you don't mind.
Philip Of course not.

Pause

Rachel How lovely this house is.
Philip It's pretty shabby. Ambrose and I always intended doing something about it, but we never did.

Pause

Rachel I have a confession to make.
Philip Oh?
Rachel I have been so jealous of you.
Philip Jealous . . . ?
Rachel Your name was always on Ambrose's lips. He told me that when your parents died he brought you up. You were so close. I had such pictures of you. Spoilt, I thought. Priggish, I thought. Did you wonder about me?
Philip Yes.
Rachel And pictured me as a scheming Italian widow.

Philip looks extremely uncomfortable. Rachel bursts out laughing

Philip, I may be Italian, or half Italian, and a widow, but I am far from scheming. How else did you picture me?
Philip Older. Not so . . .
Rachel Not so what?
Philip Not so—easy to talk to.
Rachel Thank you. We should talk easily together, you and I. We have so much in common—Ambrose, Barton, the house and the garden. When will you show me round the estate?
Philip On Monday. Can you ride?
Rachel Not well.

Philip We have a steady horse called Dolabella, who would suit you.

Rachel What a charming name—Dolabella.

Philip It was Ambrose's name for her.

Rachel Cyprian, Angus, Thunderer, Spick and Span . . .

Philip You know all the horses.

Rachel And the dogs, Brimstone, Treacle, Flare, Sammy, Joshua. Why do you look at me like that?

Philip Funny—we've only just met but I feel as if I'd known you a long time.

Rachel Tell me, Philip, were you, perhaps, just a little bit jealous of me, too?

Pause

Philip Yes.

Rachel You had no reason. We shared Ambrose's heart. I never took the part of it that was not mine. Do you think we could be friends? No—it is too early to wonder about that. When I return to Florence next week, perhaps we shall know.

Philip You are going back next week?

Rachel Yes.

Philip There is no need to hurry.

Rachel Ah, but there is. My mission here will be accomplished and I have much to do in Florence. I have to sell the villa, alas.

Philip Must you? Why?

Rachel I can no longer afford to keep it up.

Philip I see.

Rachel Let's not talk about unpleasant things. Perhaps you would ring the bell? Seecombe will have prepared the tisane tray the way I showed him by this time.

Philip pulls a bell-rope

When Ambrose and I were first married he used to drink brandy in the evening, but I soon changed that.

Philip What is tisane?

Rachel There are all kinds. It is a tea made with herbs. I make mine from a receipt given me by my mother. It soothes the nerves and helps you sleep. All through his illness Ambrose could take it when he could take nothing else.

Seecombe enters with a silver tray, with a tea-pot, cups, hot water, etc.

Thank you, Seecombe.

Seecombe places the tray on a table by her side

Philip Where on earth did that tray come from, Seecombe?

Seecombe (*coldly*) There is a great deal of silver in the family, Mr Philip. Will that be all, madam?

Rachel Yes, thank you, Seecombe. Good night.

Seecombe Good night, madam. Good night, Mr. Philip.

Seecombe goes out with dignity

Rachel giggles

Rachel You were snubbed. And rightly. (*She busies herself with the tray*) Tomorrow is Sunday?

Philip Yes.

Rachel Ambrose told me of the great box pew you had, and how naughty little Philip used to let mice loose in it.

Philip Following naughty old Ambrose's example.

Rachel What a couple of children. Here. (*She hands him a cup*) Try it.

He sips

Philip It's—it's a little bitter.

Rachel The next sip will taste less bitter. (*She pours a cup for herself*) I suppose we shall have to go to church.

Philip (*surprised*) You wish to?

Rachel Ambrose would have wished me to. I am a Catholic, but I will be able to follow the service, I think.

Philip You will create a sensation in Barton.

Rachel And after church, Mr Kendall and his daughter, Louise, come to dine—is that not so?

Philip You know everything.

Rachel Miss Louise and you are great friends. She is very pretty, Ambrose said.

Philip She's all right.

Rachel You are not very *gallant*, but perhaps Cornwall is full of pretty girls.

Philip Perhaps. I've always been too busy to bother about things like that.

Rachel You will not always be too busy. (*She puts down her cup and rises*) Good night, Philip, and thank you.

Philip Thank me—for what?

Rachel Making me welcome in your home.

Philip Must you go—it's early.

Rachel I am not a late bird like you and Ambrose. And I am tired. Coming here to Barton for the first time was a slight effort—thank you for making it so easy. Good night, Cousin Philip.

Philip Good night, Cousin Rachel.

Rachel picks up the candle and goes slowly up the stairs. She goes into her room, shutting the door behind her

The Lights fade

SCENE 4

The same. About 4.30 in the afternoon

Seecombe bustles in with a silver dish with ratafia biscuits which he puts on a table. He then goes to a cupboard which he opens and takes out some wine glasses. He is followed on by James carrying another tray with three decanters of port, sherry and madeira

Seecombe Careful with them now: they've only just seen the light o' day!

James lowers the tray on to the sideboard. He sees the dish of biscuits and picks it up curiously

James What're they?

Seecombe You put them back now, this instant.

James But what are they?

Seecombe Comfits.

James looks blank

James What d'you do with 'em?

Seecombe You eat 'em.

James gives a blank look of acknowledgement

Sweetmeats—they're taken with your sherry-madeira-wine and such. Leastways that's what madam says you do wi' 'em.

James Queer folk the gentry. Now what I fancies is a good mug of ale and . . .

There is laughter from beyond the door to the dining-room

Seecombe Never you mind: you make yerself scarce—they're comin' through.

Seecombe goes out. As he does so James takes one of the biscuits and darts out. Rachel enters with Kendall

Kendall Besides which, m'dear, all the congregation, indeed most of the county know that you came from outlandish foreign parts. For all they know Italians may be black. So many people asked me when they will have an opportunity to meet you—officially. I think you can reckon upon engagements every afternoon for at least the next four weeks.

Rachel There is nothing that I would like better, Mr Kendall, but, alas I am only a visitor to Barton and, in the circumstances . . .

Louise and Philip enter

After a brief moment Rachel joins Louise

Miss Kendall, I believe I owe you an apology. Yesterday in my enthusiasm for becoming acquainted with Barton, I unwittingly prevented Philip from calling upon you at Pelyn.

Philip goes to pour drinks

Louise No matter. He had no serious obligation in that respect.

Kendall Philip, your cousin should, by rights undertake certain social commitments as she is in this part of the world. I know that you—and Ambrose—paid little heed to such niceties—but I am sure many people in the county would be honoured to meet your Cousin Rachel.

Philip (*smiling as he hands her sherry*) They would indeed be honoured.

Rachel As I say I am merely a visitor and, in the circumstances, I feel I should leave in the morning.

Kendall So soon? You're hardly an ordinary visitor, m'dear—and had Ambrose lived Barton would have been your home.

Rachel Had Ambrose lived, Mr Kendall, a lot of things would have been otherwise. (*Pause. She changes the conversation deliberately*) Did you know that Ambrose had planned a sunken garden with a fountain—like the one we had at the villa.

Kendall Charming—where was it to be?

Rachel I'll show you—will you come with me. (*She picks up a shawl*) We had planned it down to the last detail. It was to have been the first thing we were going to do when we came back.

Rachel and Kendall go towards the door

Kendall I envy you gardeners your patience. To plant a tree and wait perhaps for years for it to bear fruit.

Rachel Ah, but when it does bear fruit—it is worth the waiting.

Rachel and Kendall go out

Louise *I'm* waiting, Phil.

Philip What for?

Louise What for?

Philip Oh, you mean yesterday afternoon. I'm sorry, but it was impossible to get away. My Cousin Rachel wished to see all the Barton acres.

Louise Oh, don't apologize. I waited about two hours, but it didn't matter.

Philip I'm really very sorry.

Louise I guessed something of the sort had kept you. I'm thankful it was nothing more serious. I thought you might have had some terrible disagreement.

Philip No. We didn't.

Louise Have you really survived so far without a clash? Tell me all.

Philip What do you mean by all?

Louise What did you say to her? How did she take it? Was she very much aghast by all you said, or did she show no sign of guilt at all?

Philip We've really had little time for talking but she is a very different person from the person I expected. You must have seen that from your brief meeting before the service.

Louise She is very beautiful.

Philip Beautiful?

Louise Yes, beautiful! Ask Father. Ask anyone. Didn't you notice how the people stared in church when she put up her veil?

Philip Of course they stared at her. There hasn't been a woman in the Ashley pew for over thirty years.

Louise Her profile is like that on a rare old coin. She makes the rest of us look like country bumpkins—or bumpkinesses—if there is such a word. Has she said much about Ambrose?

Philip Naturally.

Louise What?

Philip Ambrose told her everything.

Louise But those letters—I thought . . .

Philip (*hurriedly*) We must remember they were written when he was very ill.

Pause

Louise (*slowly*) It's not true.

Philip What isn't?

Louise You can't have changed overnight.

Philip I don't know what you're talking about.

Louise Don't you remember what you said about her last week?

Philip Of course I do; it's just that I might have been a trifle hasty. One must give her the benefit of the doubt.

Pause

Louise You've fallen in love with her.

Philip Don't be absurd.

Louise It's the only explanation.

Philip I have *not* fallen in love with her. The thing's ridiculous. She only arrived yesterday.

Louise What about Romeo and Juliet?

Philip What about them?

Louise "Whoever loved that loved not at first sight . . ."

Philip That's schoolgirl nonsense.

Louise It isn't—it's Shakespeare. I suppose it's understandable, really. You've never seen a beautiful woman before.

Philip Oh, do stop about her being beautiful.

Louise I never thought I'd watch you making a fool of yourself over a woman years too old for you.

Philip She's not old.

Louise She's thirty-five at least.

Philip For God's sake, Louise, let's talk about something else.

Louise Very well. (*Pause*) You'll be coming as usual to drive me over to Pascoes tomorrow?

Philip I'm sorry. I can't.

Louise But why? It's all arranged.

Philip I just can't, that's why.

Louise You're going somewhere with her.

Philip If you must know—I'm showing her round the village.

Louise Were you planning to let me know—or were you once more just not going to turn up?

Philip Of course I was going to let you know.

Louise I don't believe you.

Philip All right—don't.

Louise When is she going back to Italy?

Philip I don't know.

Louise The sooner the better if you ask me.

Philip I didn't ask you.

Louise (*brokenly*) Oh—Phil . . .

Philip What on earth's the matter with you, Louise? You're making a stupid scene over nothing, mountains out of molehills or some such—and now you're crying.

Louise I am *not*.

Philip All because I said I might have been mistaken about my Cousin Rachel.

Louise If you go on talking about her I shall scream.

Philip All right, scream. And I am not the one who's talking about her. You are.

Louise Phil, listen to me . . .

Rachel and Kendall are heard, off. Louise turns away

Kendall and Rachel enter

Kendall (*taking off his glasses and wiping them*) My dear Philip, I think this sunken garden is a splendid idea. One very important thing about it, though—we must persuade Mrs Ashley to stay on for a while and at least see it started.

Rachel I'm afraid that may not be possible.

Kendall Try to persuade your cousin, Philip.

Philip I'll do my best, sir.

Louise It's time we were going, Father.

Kendall No hurry, my dear. Tell me, Mrs Ashley, do you not think there is a remarkable resemblance between Philip and Ambrose?

Rachel When I first saw Cousin Philip, I thought he *was* Ambrose.

Kendall All the Ashleys bear a strong family likeness.

Rachel My father had the unmistakeable nose.

Kendall Ambrose used to say it was the ideal nose for looking down. (*He goes to the window, and puts his glasses on the window-seat*)

Rachel Philip—when we go through Ambrose's books, there may be some that Mr Kendall might like.

Philip Good idea. And I'd like you to have his walking stick, sir. You've brought it, Cousin Rachel?

Rachel I've brought everything, even to the battered old hat he used to wear in the garden. I brought that specially for you, Philip.

Louise (*abruptly*) Father, I've got a bad headache.

Kendall Have you, dear? I'm sorry. Well, we'd better be getting home. Now, Mrs Ashley, please arrange with Philip what evening you can come to supper and let us know. We're free every evening except Monday, are we not, Louise?

Louise Yes, Father.

Kendall Well, good-bye, Mrs Ashley, it's been delightful. And no more of this nonsense about hurrying back to Italy. Now you're here we're going to keep you for a while. Good-bye, Philip.

Philip Good-bye, sir.

Louise Good-bye, Mrs Ashley.
Rachel Good-bye, Miss Kendall. I look forward to dining with you very much.
Kendall Perhaps we can fix a day now.
Rachel Would Tuesday be convenient? Oh no—I forgot Philip always goes over to Lydstone on Tuesdays. Wednesday perhaps?
Kendall Capital—eh, Louise?
Louise Yes, Father.
Rachel Philip?
Philip Fine.
Kendall Very well. Till Wednesday. Come, my dear.

Louise and Kendall go out, accompanied by Philip

Rachel moves about tidying the cushions

Philip returns from the door

Rachel I'm sorry your Miss Kendall had a headache.
Philip Yes—and she's not my Miss Kendall.
Rachel Oh? I thought from something that Ambrose once said ...
Philip What?
Rachel Never mind. Philip, as I may be leaving soon, don't you think it would be a good idea to go through Ambrose's things?
Philip I'll tell Seecombe to get the trunks brought down. (*He goes to the door and calls*) Seecombe!
Seecombe (*off*) Yes, Mr Philip.

Rachel wanders around

Philip Get Mr Ambrose's trunks brought down, will you?
Seecombe (*off*) Yes, Mr Philip.

Philip returns. Rachel turns and smiles at him

Rachel I can see this is a bachelor establishment. Not a single mirror except in the bedrooms—and then only tiny ones, set at the most uncomfortable angles.
Philip Cousin Rachel?
Rachel Yes?
Philip Could you not be persuaded to stay on a little and, as Uncle Nick mentioned, just get the sunken garden started?
Rachel I shall have to think about it.
Philip I wish you would.
Rachel The trouble is I really must see Signor Rainaldi about selling the villa.
Philip Could you not write to him?
Rachel Possibly, but I would like to be there. Imagine if it were Barton that was to be sold. The villa is my home.
Philip Barton is your home.
Rachel You're very sweet, Philip, and very kind ...

There is a noise, off

Seecombe and James appear from the servants' quarters, lugging two large trunks

Philip Here by the fire, Seecombe.
Seecombe Right you are, Mr Philip, sir.
Rachel Oh, Seecombe, would you bring me the tisane tray about five?
Seecombe Very good, madam.
Rachel I'm going to cure Mr Philip of drinking India tea in the afternoon.
Seecombe Very good, madam.

Seecombe goes off with James

Rachel Shall we have a look at the books first?

Philip undoes the clasp on the first trunk and throws back the lid. Rachel kneels down in front of the trunk and starts to sort the books

Your Gardening Companion, Tuscan Gardens, Gardens of Northern Italy, The Flowers of Florence—I'd forgotten how many gardening books we had acquired. *Herbs and their Uses*—I'll give this one to you, Philip, so that you can make yourself tisane after I've gone. Shakespeare, a lovely edition. Mr Kendall would appreciate that, don't you think? More books about gardening—ah! *The Sunken Garden*, that will be useful if you do decide . . .
Philip (*interrupting*) I have decided. We're having the sunken garden.
Rachel Poetry—Lord Byron, Shelley, Keats—Ambrose loved the poetry of Keats. "In some melodious plot, Of beechen green and shadows numberless, Singest of summer in full-throated ease . . ." Andrew Marvell—"Annihilating all that's made, To a green thought in a green shade . . ." That's what we'll have in the sunken garden, Philip, "a green thought in a green shade". More and more gardening books. Here—take your book and the book for Mr Kendall. I'll go through the gardening books on my own some time. I don't know which are worth keeping—they deal mostly with Italian gardens.

She rises and hands the two books to Philip, then shuts the lid of the trunk. Philip undoes the second trunk and throws back the lid. Rachel begins to look inside, then suddenly sways and puts her hand to her eyes

Philip Cousin Rachel!

She sways against him. He puts his arm round her

Rachel I'm sorry.
Philip Here, come and sit down.
Rachel No—no, I'll be all right.
Philip We'll finish this another time.
Rachel No. (*She draws away from him, pulls herself together and kneels down by the trunk. She lifts out a jacket*) For you?
Philip I couldn't.
Rachel It was his favourite jacket. I can see him now—sitting by the fountain . . .

Philip Please, Rachel, let's leave this for another time.
Rachel No, let's get it over. I'd no idea that clothes could be so cruel.
What shall we do with them?
Philip Seecombe might have a suggestion—he's a wise old bird.
Rachel Yes. (*She reaches into the trunk and produces a battered old hat*)
This?
Philip Yes, that I will have. (*He takes it and crosses to the servants' door.
He calls*) Seecombe!
Rachel Do you never ring for him?
Philip Sometimes. Usually Ambrose and I just shouted.

Seecombe enters

Seecombe, we'd like your advice. Mr Ambrose's clothes, what shall we
do with them?
Seecombe They'd fit you, sir.
Philip No, Seecombe.
Seecombe I see. Well, Mr Philip, sir, what about giving them round to the
servants and the men on the estate? Christmas is coming and the clothes
could be a bonus on top of their usual presents.
Philip I knew I could rely on you, Seecombe.
Seecombe Yes, sir. (*To Rachel*) You look tired, madam. Shall I bring in the
tray?
Rachel Please.

Seecombe goes out

Dear Seecombe—he understands.
Philip Yes.
Rachel The clothes brought him back so vividly. I remember when I first
met him at a dinner party given by the Contessa di Paoli. It was one of
those typical Florentine occasions with everyone talking their heads off.
He sat on my right and looked—oh so desperately bored. I hadn't
heard his name properly and tried, unsuccessfully, to find a topic of
conversation that might interest him. He was polite but gave no help.
Finally, I asked him what part of England he came from and he said
Cornwall. I said I had Cornish blood and that my maiden name had
been Ashley. He looked at me as if he saw me for the first time and said,
"You must be my Cousin Rachel. I am Ambrose Ashley."

Seecombe enters with the tisane tray

Rachel smiles her thanks

Seecombe goes out

Rachel begins to prepare the tea

I asked him what he was doing in Florence and he told me he had come
for his health as the Cornish winter tried him sorely, and to look at the
gardens. "Then you must look at my garden at the Villa Sangaletti," I
said, and we arranged that he should call the following morning. Then
the hostess rose and we had no further opportunity of speech.

But he came early the next morning and I showed him over my garden . . . he was so enthusiastic and so knowledgeable. Then we sat and drank tisane just as you and I are doing, there in the sunlight. I felt a sense of well-being and happiness—I'd never known before. My first marriage had been unfortunate. Guido was so much older than I, cold and unfeeling, aloof and completely without compassion, whereas Ambrose was so warm, so understanding. I think we both knew that first morning. I know I did. After he had gone I sat on as if in a dream—a dream that was soon to become a wonderful reality. (*She puts down her cup*) I talk too much.

Philip No.

Rachel It is a great thing to be able to say, "Then I was happy". Another cup?

Philip Thank you.

Rachel Ah, it does not taste so bitter now. (*She smiles at him*)

Philip Louise was right—you are beautiful.

Rachel Am I?

Philip Very beautiful.

Rachel I am thirty-five, Philip.

Philip Really? I thought you were older.

Rachel From you I take that as a compliment.

Philip Might I ask you something?

Rachel Of course—anything.

Philip Do you really have to sell your villa?

Rachel Yes.

Philip I wish . . .

Rachel Yes?

Philip Uncle Nick was surprised that Ambrose had not made another will —in your favour.

Rachel Ah—but he did.

Philip He did?

Rachel It was never signed.

Philip Why?

Rachel He was ill. Do you mind if we do not talk about it, Philip?

Philip But we *must* talk about it.

Rachel No!

Philip I say we must.

Rachel Then I shall go to my room.

Philip No.

Rachel If you insist—I shall return to Italy tomorrow.

Philip But why? Why will you not talk about it?

Rachel I am a woman. I have my reasons. I am a very private person. I must ask you to respect that privacy.

Philip If it is simply a matter of money . . .

Rachel Money? One can always get money somehow. I could pawn my rings—or live in London and give lessons in Italian.

Philip Mrs Ambrose Ashley give lessons in Italian!

Rachel I have no false pride, Philip. Good night.

Philip Don't go!
Rachel You leave me no choice.
Philip I won't mention it again—only—don't go!
Rachel I would prefer to if you don't mind. I am suddenly very tired. It
was foolish of me to insist on going through Ambrose's things—
inanimate objects can hurt so much.
Philip I am dreadfully sorry. Please forgive me.
Rachel Of course. There is nothing to forgive. Good night.

Rachel goes slowly upstairs and into her room. The door closes

Philip swears and kicks the logs of the fire

Seecombe enters

Seecombe May I remove the tray, sir?
Philip Yes.

There is a ring at the front door

Who the hell . . .?

Seecombe goes to the door and opens it. Kendall enters

Uncle Nick!
Kendall Left my spectacles behind, always doing it.
Philip Where did you have them last?
Kendall When I came back from the garden with Mrs Ashley.
Philip Look for them, Seecombe, will you? Uncle Nick—this is providen-
tial. I must have a word with you.
Kendall Where's Mrs Ashley?
Philip Gone to her room.
Kendall A bit early, isn't it?

Seecombe goes to the window-seat

Philip She was tired.
Seecombe Here are your spectacles, sir.
Kendall Thank you, Seecombe.

Seecombe goes out with the tray

Well, Philip, in my opinion, Mrs Ashley is a fine woman. I commend
Ambrose's taste. Changed your opinion, I hope.
Philip He did make another will.
Kendall Who did?
Philip Ambrose.
Kendall How do you know?
Philip She told me. I asked her. He never signed it.
Kendall Why not?
Philip He was ill, she said.
Kendall Do you know the terms?
Philip She didn't tell me.

Kendall Extraordinary!

Philip I tried to insist but she became angry. Finally she said she could always pawn her rings and give Italian lessons.

Kendall We can't allow that.

Philip Of course not.

Kendall Why didn't he sign it? Ambrose was always so business-like.

Philip What can we do?

Kendall Make her an allowance from the estate.

Philip Would she accept it?

Kendall We can but try.

Philip How much?

Kendall Up to you, my boy.

Philip Two hundred pounds a quarter?

Kendall That's generous—but why not?

Philip Will you see about it at once?

Kendall I'll send my boy over with the deed tomorrow. Italian lessons—eh!

Philip A glass of brandy?

Kendall Thank you.

Philip goes and pours two brandies

Most extraordinary.

Both drink

Well, Philip, in a few months you'll be monarch of all you survey.

Philip On All Fools' Day. What a day to choose for a birthday.

Kendall And my duties cease.

Philip You've been the best guardian a fellow ever had.

Kendall Funny—Ambrose insisting you wait till you were twenty-five.

Philip He always said a man didn't know his own mind till twenty-five and no woman until she was thirty.

Kendall Women know their own minds in the cradle.

Philip Really, Uncle Nick!

Kendall But then you and Ambrose never knew the first thing about women. That's why I'm so glad . . .

Philip Yes?

Kendall That Mrs Ashley seems such an exceptional woman.

Philip Yes.

Kendall Ambrose could so easily have fallen a prey to the wrong sort . . . Remarkable eyes.

Philip Yes.

Kendall That's the Italian blood of course.

Philip Yes.

Kendall I'm surprised that Ambrose never sent for any of the Ashley jewellery.

Philip I'd forgotten about the jewels—very fine some of them I believe?

Kendall They're magnificent. Your grandfather was a great collector—the emeralds alone are superb.

Philip I seem to remember a famous pearl collar . . .

Kendall It's the gem of the whole lot in my opinion. Well, I must be going.
I'll get that sent round tomorrow.
Philip Good.
Kendall (*going to the door*) Louise seems a little under the weather,
poor child ...

Philip remains silent

Well, see you on Wednesday—and do give my regards to Mrs Ashley.
Philip I will. Good night, Uncle Nick, and thank you.

Kendall goes out

*Philip escorts him then returns to the room and stands for a moment in
thought. Then he runs up the stairs and taps at Rachel's door*

Rachel (*off*) Who is it?
Philip Philip.

*Pause. Then slowly the door opens and Rachel appears, her hair is down
and she wears a wrap*

Rachel Yes, Philip?
Philip I—I ...
Rachel Why do you stare at me like that?
Philip I've never seen a woman in undress before.
Rachel (*smiling*) What was it you wanted?
Philip I just hoped you weren't cross with me—that's all.
Rachel No, Philip, I'm not cross with you.

*Rachel leans forward and kisses Philip on the cheek, then quickly shuts the
door*

*Philip stands for a moment and then gleefully bounds down the stairs,
smiling happily*

The Lights fade

SCENE 5

The same. Late afternoon the next day

The bell rings at the front door. Seecombe emerges and admits Kendall

Kendall Mr Philip in?
Seecombe Yes, sir. Just back from riding, sir. I'll let him know you're here.
Kendall Thanks.

Seecombe goes upstairs and off

Kendall takes out a document and studies it

Seecombe reappears upstairs

Seecombe (*descending*) Will you take a glass of wine, sir? Mr Philip won't
be a moment.

Kendall No, thank you, Seecombe.

As Seecombe exits, Philip appears upstairs

Philip (*descending*) Hallo, Uncle Nick.

Kendall Thought I'd bring this over myself. (*He hands the document to Philip who reads it quickly and hands it back*)

Philip Thank you. Yes. Very well put.

Kendall How is Mrs Ashley?

Philip Fine. We've been out riding.

Kendall I thought it might be a good idea if I had a word with her— (*indicating the deed*)—about this.

Philip Oh.

Kendall I thought the reason why she refused to disclose the terms of the unsigned will might be—er—reasons of delicacy—you being the heir.

Philip I see.

Kendall She might talk to me more freely.

Philip Shall I call her?

Kendall If you would.

Philip And then vanish. Is that the idea?

Kendall Precisely.

Philip Right. (*He goes upstairs and knocks at Rachel's door*) Cousin Rachel . . .

Rachel (*off*) Yes?

Philip Uncle Nick is here. He'd like a word with you.

Rachel (*off*) Of course.

Philip makes a thumbs-up gesture to Kendall and goes off upstairs. Pause. Rachel emerges from her room and comes down the stairs

Mr Kendall—what a pleasant surprise.

Kendall I hear you have been out riding.

Rachel Yes. What a beautiful part of the world. I am more than ever proud of my Cornish blood.

Kendall Mrs Ashley—I had a talk with Philip yesterday.

Rachel Oh yes? Won't you sit down? (*She sits*)

Kendall (*sitting*) Thank you. Mrs Ashley, Philip and I wish you to do Barton a favour . . .

Rachel But of course. I have already promised to give away the prizes at the Harvest Festival.

Kendall Perhaps you would be so kind as to glance at this?

He hands her the document, which she reads quickly

Rachel Mr Kendall . . . (*She puts her hands across her eyes*)

Kendall It's the least Barton can do for you.

Rachel I won't deny it will be very welcome. My first husband left me such a legacy of debt. I am most grateful to Philip—and to you.

Kendall If Ambrose had signed the other will . . .

Rachel So Philip told you . . .

Kendall Yes.

Rachel I'm afraid I was—not as kind to him as I should have been. I was—well—I was embarrassed.

Kendall Perfectly understandable, dear lady, perfectly.

Rachel Thank you.

Kendall He had left you everything?

Rachel For my lifetime or until I remarried—then to Philip and his heirs.

Kendall I see.

Rachel Now let us talk of something else. How is your daughter's headache?

Kendall Much better.

Rachel She's a very pretty girl.

Kendall I think so.

Rachel Everyone must think so. She'd be a sensation in Florence with her delicate English colouring.

Seecombe enters

Seecombe Shall I bring in the tray, madam?

Rachel Please do, Seecombe. And call Mr Philip. You'll stay, will you not, Mr Kendall?

Kendall Seecombe offered me a glass of sherry earlier.

Rachel I'll pour it for you. (*She pours the wine*)

During the next few lines, Seecombe goes upstairs to call Philip, then descends and goes off to get the tray

I have never been to a Harvest Festival.

Kendall It's quite an occasion here. The tense rivalry about who has grown the largest pumpkin . . .

Rachel I do not think we have them in Italy.

Kendall I'm glad you have promised to give away the prizes. The Festival is still a month away, so you will not be leaving Barton immediately.

Rachel The temptation to stay for a little and start the sunken garden is, I admit, very great.

Kendall Good! I hope it may prove overwhelming.

Philip appears and comes down the stairs

Rachel meets him at the foot

Rachel Philip—my dear Philip—what a sweet and generous gesture.

Philip Oh, it's nothing.

Rachel It is a great deal. (*She presses his arm and turns back to Kendall*)

Kendall I think we are going to win, Philip.

Philip Oh?

Kendall The temptation to stay and start the sunken garden is proving too strong for Mrs Ashley.

Philip Splendid.

Seecombe enters with the tray and brings it to Rachel

Rachel Thank you, Seecombe. Yes, I am weakening. How long do you think it will take, Philip?

Philip Could my estate men manage, do you think, or should we need to call in experts?

Rachel Your head gardener Tamlyn is very good. I think if he and I drew up the plans we could manage with the under-gardeners and the men from the estate.

Philip It would take several months. The days are beginning to draw in.

Rachel Perhaps if I stayed until Christmas . . .

Kendall Capital. Barton Christmases are quite occasions.

Rachel And then perhaps came back in the spring?

Kendall And the sunken garden should be ready for Philip's coming-of-age in April. I'll drink to that. (*He does so*)

Rachel hands Philip a cup of tisane

Rachel You are having a big celebration?

Philip No. The celebrations will be at Christmas.

Rachel I shall look forward to Christmas.

Kendall (*suddenly*) Isn't this pleasant? You know, Mrs Ashley, you supply the one ingredient needed to make Barton ideal.

Rachel And what is that?

Kendall A woman. Do you not agree, Philip?

Philip Certainly.

Rachel You are very charming, both of you.

Kendall A house is not a home without a woman.

Rachel You are fortunate in having a daughter.

Kendall Louise is a child still—completely absorbed in her dogs and horses. Do you hunt, Mrs Ashley?

Rachel I'm afraid not.

Kendall We must see about that. I have a mare that might suit you.

Philip My cousin found Dolabella much to her liking.

Kendall Dear old Dolabella—still, she must try my Angelica.

Philip I think we could provide Mrs Ashley with something suitable.

Kendall No doubt, no doubt.

Philip I've been thinking of buying some new hunters.

Kendall The price of a good hunter is staggering these days.

Philip My Cousin Rachel needs a horse that she likes and likes her. I'm sure you'll agree to that.

Kendall That is why I suggested Angelica. She's as gentle as a lamb.

Rachel is quietly amused by this exchange. She watches covertly over her tea-cup

Philip Angelica is past it, Uncle Nick.

Kendall Nonsense. Now, your Dolabella . . .

Seecombe enters with letters on a salver

Seecombe The post has come, Mr Philip.

Philip takes the letters from the salver

Philip Thank you, Seecombe.

Seecombe Have you finished, madam?
Rachel Yes. You may take the tray.
Seecombe Thank you, madam.

Seecombe takes the tray and goes

Philip hands two letters to Rachel

Philip Two for you—from Italy.
Rachel Ah—from my faithful Signor Rainaldi. (*She rises*) If you will forgive me. These letters will probably need my immediate attention. Good-bye, Mr Kendall, and thank you.
Philip Supper will be in half-an-hour.
Rachel I am not likely to forget. Seecombe told me we are having guinea fowl—a particular favourite of mine—and of Ambrose.

Rachel goes upstairs and into her room

Kendall Delightful woman.
Philip What can he be writing about?
Kendall Who? Signor Rainaldi? Business, I suppose.
Philip I couldn't stand the fellow. I expect he's trying to get her to go back to Florence.
Kendall Well—she's staying here until Christmas at any rate. No more of this talk of going to London and giving Italian lessons.
Philip No, thank God!
Kendall I have promised Louise to take her up to London before Christmas. She will stay with an old school friend.
Philip Did she tell you about the will?
Kendall Yes. I was right. It was a matter of delicacy. Ambrose had left her everything for her lifetime.
Philip I see.
Kendall Or until she remarried.
Philip She's not likely to do that.
Kendall Why not? An attractive woman like that? She's not likely to remain a widow long.
Philip She was devoted to Ambrose.
Kendall My dear Philip—however devoted one may have been to one's partner—and I was devoted to my dear Alison, there comes a time . . . However, we shall see. Well, I must be going. Any message for Louise?
Philip Oh, the usual—looking forward to seeing her and all that.
Kendall What a casual generation you are. Now, in my day . . . Well, good-bye, my boy.
Philip Good-bye, Uncle Nick.
Kendall (*going*) I should forget that Dolabella if I were you—Angelica is just what Mrs Ashley needs.

He goes off

Philip stands looking after him for a moment

Philip (*calling*) Seecombe!

Seecombe enters

Seecombe Mr Philip?

Philip Tell George to bring Cyprian round in the morning. I am going to ride into Bodmin. I hear that old Stebbins has some promising young hunters.

Seecombe Very good, Mr Philip.

Philip Oh and Seecombe—a bottle of the best claret with supper. Better decant it now and have another one ready.

Seecombe Very good, Mr Philip.

Philip By the way, Seecombe, Mrs Ashley has decided to stay on for a bit —at least until Christmas.

Seecombe That is excellent news, Mr Philip. If I may make so bold, sir, madam has made a great impression in the Servants' Hall.

Philip I'm sure she has.

Seecombe We are all agreed, sir, that a mistress has been needed at Barton for a long time.

Philip (*quoting*) "A house is not a home without a woman"—that's what Mr Kendall said.

Seecombe Mr Kendall should know, sir, he's been a widower these ten years. When Miss Louise marries, he'll find himself very lonely. Will that be all, sir?

Philip Yes, Seecombe, that will be all.

Seecombe goes

Philip is left scowling

Uncle Nick . . .

The Lights fade

SCENE 6

The same. Christmas afternoon

James is struggling with a Christmas tree in a tub, to get it into position, below the stairs. Seecombe, who holds a list and a pile of cards, supervises

There are now one or two mirrors hanging in the Hall

Seecombe James, the fourth branch on the right is bent.

James, none too sure of his arithmetic, points to each branch in turn as Seecombe counts to him

One—two—three—four! Yes, that one. Raise it a touch. Gently, boy, gently! The tree must seem to be standing as nature placed it. Oh, and do be careful not to stamp on the berries . . .

James Sorry, Mr Seecombe, sir.

Seecombe Now leave it. Come away. Right away. One further movement and the whole effect is spoiled. My! That's beautiful! Now, boy, the supper will start as usual at five o'clock. The trestles are already up and laid?

James Yes, Mr Seecombe, sir.

Seecombe Then here's the seating order. (*He hands him the list and pile of cards*)

James What do I do with these?

Seecombe The names of all the guests are on those pieces of paper, boy. You just place them on the appropriate platters.

James But you forget, Mr Seecombe, there are folks as can't read.

Seecombe I forget nothing, James. I have made quite certain that those who can't read have neighbours who can. Now just do as you are told and put them on the appropriate platters.

James But you forget, Mr Seecombe, I'm one of them as can't read.

Seecombe Oh damn you, boy. (*He takes them back*) Give them here. I'll do it myself.

James rushes off to the servants' quarters. Philip enters from upstairs

Philip That's a fine tree, Seecombe.

Seecombe Glad you like it, Mr Philip.

Philip Where's the mistress?

Seecombe Madam is in the kitchen, sir. Cook is a trifle behind, I'm afraid.

Philip Have they started to arrive yet?

Seecombe Yes, sir. The long barn is filling up already. William and Thomas are serving ale—and sweet sherry for the ladies.

Philip How many will we be?

Seecombe About seventy, sir.

Philip A good turn-out!

Seecombe Yes, sir, the whole of Barton.

Philip Excellent! Now, when Mr Kendall and Miss Louise arrive, we shall have a glass of wine here and when everything is quite ready, will you ring the bell and we'll come along to the barn?

Seecombe Very good, Mr Philip.

Philip The presents—all organized?

Seecombe Yes, sir, yours and madam's.

Philip Madam's?

Seecombe Madam has arranged a personal gift for everyone on the estate, sir.

Philip Good heavens!

Seecombe Most particular she was that no-one should be left out. Madam was—er—good enough to consult me in the matter, sir.

Philip Very wise of her.

Seecombe Quite so, sir.

Rachel enters from the servants' quarters. She is laughing

Rachel I didn't know there *could* be so many mince-pies. Your tree looks beautiful, Seecombe.

Seecombe Thank you, madam.

Seecombe goes out to the servants' quarters

Philip You look beautiful, too, Rachel.
Rachel Are you implying that I resemble the Christmas tree?
Philip No. Come here—I've something for you.
Rachel I hope you haven't been extravagant.
Philip No. The extravagant one was my grandfather.
Rachel What do you mean?
Philip Shut your eyes.
Rachel What *is* the mystery?
Philip Shut your eyes, Rachel.

She does so. He takes a wonderful pearl collar from his pocket and clasps it round her neck

Now you may open them.
Rachel Philip—what have you . . . (*She goes to one of the mirrors which now hang in the Hall, looks in it and gasps*) Philip!
Philip It's the Ashley pearl collar. Quite famous, I believe.
Rachel For *me*?
Philip Who else?
Rachel I—I don't know what to say.
Philip There's no need to say anything.
Rachel It's exquisite. I've always longed for pearls—I've never owned any —and now this. Oh, Philip, and all I have for you are these links . . .

She hands him a small box, which he opens

Philip I shall wear them always.
Rachel Such a little thing.
Philip They're beautiful.
Rachel (*fingering the collar*) I feel like a queen.
Philip I'm glad.
Rachel The pearls—I . . . (*She stops*)
Philip Yes?
Rachel The pearls I have seen—the ones worn by my friends in Florence— were not nearly as fine as these.
Philip My grandfather—and yours—knew a great deal about jewellery. The Ashley collection is quite famous.
Rachel Where is it? I'd love to see it.
Philip In the bank.
Rachel What a pity! Jewels should be worn—did you know that if pearls are not worn they die?
Philip No.
Rachel I shall not let these die.

There is the sound of a carriage drawing up

Philip That will be Uncle Nick and Louise.

Philip goes through the main door

Rachel again goes to the mirror and fingers the pearls

Kendall (*off*) Hello, Philip—merry Christmas.

Philip (*off*) Merry Christmas, Uncle Nick—Louise.
Louise (*off*) Merry Christmas, Philip.

Kendall, Louise and Philip enter. Louise is carrying two parcels

Kendall Ah, Mrs Ashley—merry Christmas to you. (*His manner to her has changed. It is cold*)
Rachel Merry Christmas, Mr Kendall, and to you, Louise.

Louise murmurs something. Both she and Kendall suddenly notice the pearl collar

Isn't it beautiful? From Philip.
Kendall (*slowly*) The Ashley collar . . .
Rachel I've never seen one like it.
Kendall No. It's unique.
Rachel It has a history!
Kendall Yes. Each pearl is perfect, and perfectly matched. They took many years to collect. A famous jeweller at the French Court designed and made it. It is the best thing in the Ashley collection.
Rachel I told Philip I did not know how to thank him.
Philip Wear it—that's all I ask. Uncle Nick—Louise, your presents are in the long barn.
Louise These are for you, Mrs Ashley, and you, Philip. (*She hurriedly thrusts the parcels at Philip*)
Philip Thank you. We'll put them by the tree. Rachel, I hear that you have presents for everyone on the estate.
Rachel Only little things.
Philip It was a very generous thought. Just like you, wasn't it, Uncle Nick?
Kendall Yes . . .

Seecombe enters, with an apron

Seecombe Excuse me, madam, but cook says would you be so good as to spare her a few moments? Here's your apron, madam.
Rachel Of course. Nothing wrong, I hope?
Seecombe No, madam. I gather it's the matter of the spice in some sauce.
Rachel Excuse me.

Rachel goes out with Seecombe

Kendall The Ashley collar . . .
Philip Yes—doesn't it suit her?
Kendall You got it out of the bank?
Philip Yes. Old Couch was a bit difficult to start with, but I got it.
Kendall He had no right to give it to you.
Philip Why not? It's mine.
Kendall Not until April the first.
Philip Really, Uncle Nick . . . Sherry?
Kendall Thank you.

Philip pours out a drink

I'm glad of this opportunity of speaking to you.

Philip You look very grave. Is anything the matter? (*He gives Kendall his drink*)

Kendall I'm afraid so. I've had a letter from Mr Couch, Philip.

Philip About the collar?

Kendall No. When did you get it?

Philip Yesterday.

Kendall This was written the day before. As is very right and proper, he believes it his duty to inform me that Mrs Ashley is several hundred pounds overdrawn on her account.

Philip Oh?

Kendall I don't understand it. She can't have many expenses here. She is living as your guest, so her needs are met. The only thing that occurs to me is that she must be sending money out of the country.

Philip There must be some mistake. She is very generous. You heard her say she has given a present to everyone on the estate. That cannot be done for a few shillings.

Kendall Twenty pounds would pay for them a dozen times over. They could not account for such a large overdraft.

Philip She has spent money on the house. The Blue Room has new hangings—and about time too.

Kendall The fact remains the sum we agreed to pay her quarterly has been trebled, nearly quadrupled by the amount she has drawn. What are we to decide for the future?

Philip Treble, quadruple the amount we give her now.

Kendall Philip!

Philip Uncle Nick—it is Christmas Day and we are boring Louise.

Kendall A lady of quality living in London could not fritter away so much.

Philip There may be debts of which we know nothing. She may have creditors, pressing her for money, in Florence. I want you to increase her allowance to cover the overdraft.

Kendall And the collar?

Philip What of it? No harm can come to it in her keeping.

Kendall I am not so sure.

Philip What are you suggesting?

Kendall It would fetch a considerable price.

Philip Uncle Nick—if you dare . . .

Kendall You know Louise and I have been in London?

Philip If you dare suggest that my Cousin Rachel . . .

Kendall (*interrupting*) Tell him, Louise.

Louise Oh, Father—must I?

Kendall Yes, my dear, you must.

Louise Philip—when I was in London I stayed with my great friend Vanessa Dudley.

Philip Well?

Louise She and her parents—her father is in the Diplomatic Service— lived in Florence at one time. They heard that Ambrose had married the Contessa Sangaletti.

Philip Go on.

Louise Oh, Philip, I don't want to.

Philip Say what you have to say and have done with it.

Louise Her mother told me that they were horrified. She—Mrs Ashley, I mean—and her first husband were notorious for their extravagance.

Kendall Not only for their extravagance. For loose living.

Philip Filthy gossip.

Louise The tradesmen were never paid. She gave enormous parties and wore the most wonderful pearls.

Philip Ah, that proves your friends are liars. She never had any pearls until today. She told me so.

Kendall Be that as it may—I must ask you to return the collar. It must be put back in the bank with the rest of the collection.

Philip Return the collar? Impossible! I gave it to her as a Christmas present. It is the last thing in the world I would do.

Kendall Then I must speak to her about it.

Philip I'll be damned if you do.

Kendall (*altering his tone*) Come, Philip, you are very young and very impressionable. I quite understand that you wish to give your cousin a present—but not the Ashley collar.

Philip She has a right to it. If Ambrose had lived . . .

Kendall Ah, yes—if Ambrose had lived. But not now. The jewels remain in trust for your wife, Philip. And that is another reason why it must be returned. The collar has a significance of its own which some of the older tenants at dinner today will know about and talk about. An Ashley allows his bride to wear it on her wedding day as her sole adornment. This is just the sort of thing which causes gossip. I am sure Mrs Ashley would want to avoid such gossip.

Philip Rubbish!

Rachel appears in the doorway

The others do not notice her

Kendall Nevertheless that collar must be returned to the bank. I repeat—it is not yours to give—yet. And if you will not ask Mrs Ashley to return it, then I shall.

They glare at each other. Rachel comes forward

Rachel I am sorry—I could not help overhearing.

Kendall Mrs Ashley . . .

Rachel It's perfectly all right, Mr Kendall. Please do not be embarrassed. It was dear of Philip to let me wear the pearls tonight and quite right of you to ask for their return.

Philip No, Rachel! No!

She unclasps the collar and hands it to Kendall

Kendall (*taking it*) Thank you, Mrs Ashley. You understand the collar is part of the Trust and Philip had no business to take it from the bank. But young men are headstrong.

Rachel Do you need wrapping for it?
Kendall Thank you, no. My handkerchief will do.

Kendall wraps the collar in his handkerchief and puts it in his pocket. The bell sounds

Rachel Ah, all is ready. Shall we go in?
Philip Uncle Nick—will you go on in with Louise. I wish to speak with my Cousin Rachel.

Kendall bows. Louise takes Kendall's arm and they go off

God damn him and send him to hell!
Rachel Hush. You mustn't say such things.
Philip I wanted you to wear it. I wanted you to keep it always.
Rachel I am very proud to have worn it this once.
Philip He's ruined it all, all I had planned.
Rachel You're behaving like a child, Philip.
Philip I'm twenty-five all but three blasted months. Don't you know why I wanted you to wear the collar?
Rachel Because Ambrose would have given it to me.
Philip (*slowly*) Yes.
Rachel I understand and I'm very grateful.

The bell goes again

We're keeping them waiting. (*She kisses him on the lips*) Come!

Rachel takes Philip's arm and pulls him with her towards the door. The Lights fade to a Black-out, and—

the CURTAIN *falls*

ACT II

Scene 1

The same. Three months later, evening

It is Philip's birthday. Kendall is pacing up and down. Seecombe stands by

Seecombe Seems hard to realize that Mr Philip is twenty-five today. Seems only yesterday Mr Ambrose brought him here—a mite not two years old.

Kendall Yes.

Seecombe Pity the sunken garden's not finished for the occasion but the frosts were something cruel.

Kendall Yes.

Seecombe Miss Louise is well, I hope, sir?

Kendall Yes.

Seecombe I was saying to the mistress only the other day that we hadn't seen her since Christmas.

Kendall Yes.

Seecombe (*giving up*) Well, if there's nothing you're wanting . . .

Kendall (*rousing himself*) Nothing, thank you, Seecombe.

Seecombe Thank you, sir. I don't suppose Mr Philip will be long.

Seecombe goes out to the servants' quarters

Kendall continues pacing

Philip enters from the outer door

Kendall Where the devil have you been?

Philip Swimming.

Kendall In this weather? You're mad.

Philip The sea is clean. It's a kind of second baptism. I'm glad you've come.

Kendall You won't be when I've finished.

Philip I suppose you've been to the bank?

Kendall Yes.

Philip Well?

Kendall Why have you removed the Ashley collection? All of it.

Philip That's my business. The jewels are my property now and I can do what I like with it.

Kendall What are you going to do?

Philip That again is my business. You are no longer my Trustee. I am of age.

Kendall Is Mrs Ashley behind all this?

Philip No.
Kendall I don't believe you.
Philip As you wish.
Kendall Philip—what are you doing?
Philip What should have been done long ago.
Kendall And what is that?
Philip Rendering unto Caesar the things that are Caesar's.
Kendall I don't understand you.
Philip You will. This morning I went to see Jeremy Trewin.
Kendall That lawyer in Bodmin?
Philip Yes.
Kendall Why?
Philip To draw up a Deed of Gift.
Kendall A Deed of Gift?
Philip I am doing what Ambrose would have done if he had lived. I have given Barton, the house, all that it contains, and the estate, to my Cousin Rachel for her lifetime.
Kendall Philip!
Philip They are rightfully hers.
Kendall Dear God!
Philip I have not told her yet. I intend to do so this evening.
Kendall You're insane.
Philip I shall stay on at a salary and manage the estate for her.
Kendall Philip—you can't do this.
Philip I've done it. It's all signed, sealed and witnessed. It's watertight, Uncle Nick. You can do nothing.
Kendall You fool. You besotted young fool. You're infatuated with the woman. A woman whose name is a by-word in Florence.

Philip hits him. Kendall staggers and collapses on to a chair. Philip pours a drink and takes it to him

Philip Hey. I'm sorry, Uncle Nick. But I won't have anyone saying a word against her.

Kendall drinks

Kendall (*painfully*) It is hers absolutely?
Philip Unless she remarries.
Kendall I see. Can she sell any part of it?
Philip No. Ambrose would have wished to keep the estate intact.
Kendall Philip—my dear boy—I implore you . . .
Philip It's no good, Uncle Nick. This place belongs to my Cousin Rachel— to Ambrose's wife.
Kendall Have you ever thought of making her your wife?
Philip Uncle Nick!
Kendall People are talking, Philip. She's been here nearly a year.
Philip And who was eager for her to stay? You.
Kendall I was mistaken in her.
Philip You *are* mistaken in her.

Kendall No, Philip, my eyes are open. Poor Ambrose. Poor Philip.

Philip We can do without your pity.

Kendall Both of you absolutely ignorant of women. How could you be expected to withstand the wiles of one such as Mrs Ashley?

Philip You talk like someone in some vulgar novelette.

Kendall Philip—can't you *see*—can't you at least try to see? Are you so blind? She failed to get what she wanted from Ambrose—so she came here and got it from you.

Philip She knows nothing about it—nothing.

Kendall She's been very clever. It's all been most carefully planned and you've fallen straight into her trap.

Philip I have nothing more to say.

Kendall Well, I have. And after today I shall not be coming to Barton. And I will see that Louise follows my example. The Kendalls and the Ashleys have been friends for many generations but all things have to end. I will not return to your house—Ambrose's house—her house, now that you are sexually infatuated and like an impetuous young fool you've made it over to a scheming woman with a dubious background, who is ten years older than yourself. You have been swindled, Philip, my lad, and one day you will realize it. One day—and one day soon, she will have no further use for you, and you'll be homeless and penniless. Don't expect any sympathy from me, Philip—you won't get it. Everyone will laugh at you and say it serves you right.

Philip Have you finished?

Kendall Yes.

Philip Good.

Louise enters

Louise Happy birthday, Philip.

Philip Thank you.

Louise I thought you might be here, Father. Philip, we'll bring your present tomorrow—I rode over so I couldn't carry it.

Kendall I'm afraid we won't be coming over tomorrow, Louise.

Louise Why ever not? We haven't been here for ages. Have you two been quarrelling?

Philip No.

Kendall Yes.

Louise Well, stop it, then. It's Philip's birthday. No one should quarrel on their birthday.

Philip Thank you, Louise.

Louise We'll look in after dinner tomorrow, Philip. Just for a few minutes. Come along, Father.

Kendall stalks out of the room

Don't worry, Phil. I'll make him come.

Philip It will be for the last time, Louise.

Louise Why?

Philip Ask him.

Louise I'll ask him after tomorrow. We'll pretend that tomorrow is still your birthday. You look very angry, Philip.
Philip I am very angry, Louise.
Louise I must go, it's getting late.
Philip Yes.
Louise Till tomorrow.
Philip I notice you don't ask after my Cousin Rachel.
Louise No. Should I?

Louise goes out. There is a pause, then Rachel comes out of her room and down the stairs

Rachel I thought I heard voices.
Philip The Kendalls.
Rachel Why didn't you let me know, it's so long since we saw them.
Philip They were only here very briefly.
Rachel I am not as popular as I was. I wonder what could have set them against me. (*She seats herself on the sofa*)
Philip Uncle Nick's an old fool.
Rachel No, he isn't. Strange though—he liked me very well—he even flirted with me a little bit—at Christmas—perhaps he thought I had designs on him. Did they bring you a present?
Philip They're bringing it tomorrow.
Rachel Ah, then I will ask him what I have done to offend him.
Philip (*sitting beside her*) You have done nothing. It is me he is angry with.
Rachel Angry with you? Why?
Philip Let's not talk about him. It's my birthday.
Rachel We should have had a party.
Philip I'd rather be alone with you. (*He moves close to her*)
Rachel You should be surrounded by people of your own age, Philip, not dancing attendance on old women.
Philip You're not old. You never will be old.
Rachel I found a grey hair this morning. Look.
Philip I can't see it.
Rachel Look carefully.

They are very close

Seecombe enters carrying a tray with two glasses and a bottle of champagne

Philip and Rachel move apart. Philip rises

Seecombe The champagne, sir. (*He puts it on the sideboard*)
Philip Thank you, Seecombe.
Seecombe We will be drinking your health in the Hall, sir.
Philip Thank you. But you must have a glass with us, too, mustn't he, Rachel?
Rachel Of course. Where would Mr Philip be without you, Seecombe?
Seecombe (*taking an extra glass from the sideboard*) Very good of you, I'm sure, madam. (*He opens the champagne and pours three glasses*) Your health, Mr Philip.

Rachel Philip . . .

They drink

Philip Thank you.

Seecombe My old mother used to say "It's your birthday, may all your wishes come true . . ."

Rachel And did they?

Seecombe She tried to make them come true if she could. We were very poor so I used not to wish for anything unusual.

Rachel Very wise, Seecombe. Have you wished, Philip?

Philip Yes.

Rachel I hope you are as wise as Seecombe.

Seecombe I have a small gift for you, Mr Philip—a personal gift.

Philip How kind of you, Seecombe, but . . .

Seecombe (*calling*) James!

James, who has evidently been expecting the call, enters, carrying a picture. He gives it to Seecombe who hands it to Philip. James goes

Sir, this is only a trifle. A small memento of many years devoted service to the family. I hope you will not be offended and that I have not taken any liberty in assuming that you might be pleased to accept it as a gift.

Philip This is very fine indeed. So fine in fact that I shall hang it in a place of honour.

Seecombe Oh, sir. Do you consider, sir, that the likeness does me justice? Or has the artist given something of a harshness to the features? Especially the nose. I am not altogether satisfied.

Philip Perfection in a portrait is impossible, Seecombe. This is as near to it as we shall get. Speaking for myself I could not be more delighted.

Seecombe Then, Mr Philip, that is all that matters.

Philip Will you bring in the basket, Seecombe?

Seecombe Very good, sir.

Seecombe replaces his glass and goes out

Rachel What's this?

Philip A surprise.

Rachel A nice one?

Philip I think you'll like it.

Rachel I love champagne. My first husband and I . . .

Philip Yes?

Rachel He was very fond of it too. Poor Guido. Such a dreadful accident.

Philip He died in an accident?

Rachel He had a young horse. Something frightened it and it bolted. My husband was flung against a wall. Thank God it was instantaneous.

Philip Did you ever know any people called Dudley in Florence?

Rachel Not that I can remember. Why?

Philip Oh, nothing. Louise said she had some friends there called Dudley.

Rachel No—I never met them.

Seecombe enters, carrying a large wicker hamper

Seecombe Where do you want this, sir?

Philip indicates

Will that be all, Mr Philip?
Philip Yes. Good night, Seecombe.
Seecombe Good night, sir. Good night, madam.
Rachel Good night.

Seecombe goes out

Now let me guess.
Philip You never will.
Rachel Something to eat?
Philip No.
Rachel Something to drink?
Philip No.
Rachel Something to wear?
Philip I hope so. (*He takes a folded document out of his pocket*) I want you
    to take this and read it in the morning.
Rachel (*taking it*) You're being very mysterious. (*She unfolds it*)
Philip No, not now. In the morning.
Rachel Very well. (*She puts the document into a pocket*)

Philip pours out two more glasses

To you again, dear Philip.
Philip May my wishes come true.
Rachel May your wishes come true.
Philip Amen.
Rachel I only hope they are wishes that your friends can help come true.
Philip I have few friends.
Rachel I'm your friend, Philip.

She puts out her hand and draws him down beside her. It is quite dark outside.
They sit in a pool of light

Philip Every day you grow more and more beautiful.
Rachel That's the champagne talking.
Philip It's true.
Rachel It must be the Cornish air. I shall be sorry to go, Philip.
Philip You're not going.
Rachel But I must. Rainaldi wrote . . .
Philip (*interrupting*) Don't let's speak of him tonight.
Rachel Very well.
Philip How soft your hand is and so small. I believe I could hide both
    your hands in one of mine.
Rachel Something to wear, you said. A gown?
Philip No.
Rachel And the surprise is for me?
Philip Yes.
Rachel It should be for you, it's your birthday.

He pours champagne and hands her a glass

(*Dreamily*) Look at the bubbles.
Philip What did you do on your twenty-fifth birthday?
Rachel I forget. It's so long ago.
Philip Ten years.
Rachel A lifetime. You were still a schoolboy. Did you like it at Harrow?
Philip I always used to hate leaving Barton but when I got there—yes, I suppose I liked it.
Rachel I never went to school. My mother gave me lessons. Your hair wants cutting, Philip.
Philip I know.
Rachel Why—it's wet.
Philip I've been swimming.
Rachel You must be mad—in this weather?
Philip That's what Uncle Nick said.
Rachel I wonder what put him against me . . .
Philip Nobody.
Rachel Oh yes, somebody.
Philip It doesn't matter. He doesn't matter.
Rachel He's your guardian.
Philip He was. Drink up your champagne.
Rachel I shall be foxed—as Ambrose used to say.

They laugh—they are not drunk but relaxed and happy

Philip I wish this evening could go on for ever.
Rachel I wish you'd open the hamper.
Philip Very well, then. Close your eyes.

She does so. He opens the hamper and takes out the pearl collar, which he clasps round her neck

Rachel Philip—what are . . .?
Philip Open them.

She opens her eyes and her fingers go to her neck

Rachel Philip—the pearl collar!
Philip Yes! No-one can take it away from you now.

She jumps to her feet and rushes to a mirror

Rachel My collar! My lovely, lovely collar!

Philip joins her. She puts her arms round him and they embrace

(*Muffled*) I said I didn't mind. I did, Philip, I did. When I took it off I felt naked.
Philip Damn him!
Rachel They're like silk against my skin. (*She draws away from him*)
Philip Come back to the sofa. (*He pulls her with him*) Close your eyes.
Rachel Again?

Philip Again.

She does so. Excitedly he delves into the hamper and brings out handfuls of jewels which he showers on her. She opens her eyes

Rachel Philip!

Philip Do you like sapphires? They're yours. And emeralds—look at these rubies—and the diamonds. Here's a bracelet—here's another—this was my grandmother's necklace—more sapphires—this tiara is all emeralds. This ring is supposed to have belonged to Mary Stuart and this one to Nelly Gwynn . . .

Rachel Philip, I'm dreaming . . .

Philip They're all yours—and I'm all yours, dearest, dearest Rachel.

Rachel Philip . . .

He buries his face in her lap

Philip I love you—I love you.

Rachel Hush . . .

He lifts his face

Philip It's true.

Rachel You know me so little.

Philip I know you are the most wonderful, most beautiful woman in the world.

Rachel Dear Philip. Sweet Philip.

Philip My wish—make my wish come true.

Rachel But—Philip . . .

Philip The only wish I could have, will ever have—you know what it is—you can't not know . . .

Rachel (*slowly*) Yes, I think I know.

Philip Rachel.

Rachel Philip, are you sure?

Philip Sure? It's the only thing I'm sure of in this world.

Rachel I'll be your first . . . ?

Philip And only. Rachel, I'm so in love, I'm drowning. Help me.

Rachel My dear . . .

She rises, scattering jewels and holds out her hand. He scrambles to his feet

Turn out the lamp.

She picks up a candle, lights it, and starts up the stairs. He turns out the lamp

At the top of the stairs she stops and looks down at him, then she goes into her room, leaving the door open

The candle flickers

Philip stumbles up the stairs and goes into her room

The door closes. The Lights fade

SCENE 2

The same. Afternoon, the following day

Seecombe is pottering. Philip enters

Philip Mrs Ashley back?

Seecombe No, sir.

Philip I don't understand it. She didn't tell me—er—last night that she was going into Bodmin.

Seecombe She ordered the carriage early this morning, Mr Philip, when you were out seeing the men.

Philip Thank you, Seecombe.

Seecombe They're taking their time with that bridge over the sunken garden, aren't they, sir?

Philip Rome wasn't built in a day, Seecombe.

Seecombe No, sir.

Philip Mr Kendall and Miss Louise may be looking in, Miss Louise told me she had a birthday present for me.

Seecombe Shall I bring in the sherry, sir?

Philip No, champagne. I'll ring.

Seecombe Very good, sir. The champagne last night was to your liking?

Philip It was excellent.

Seecombe goes

Philip goes and pours a generous brandy, drinks it and pours another, which he swallows quickly. A carriage is heard approaching

Philip hurries out

Louise's voice is heard off

Philip, looking glum, re-enters with Louise who is chattering brightly, and Kendall who looks grim. Louise carries a parcel which is obviously a gun

Louise I knew you wanted one of the new guns, so I sent to London for it. It only arrived yesterday—and here it is. With all our best wishes. (*She hands it to him*)

Philip Thank you, Louise, it is very kind of you. (*He rings*)

Louise Fancy you ringing. You always used to shout.

Philip I ring when I remember.

Louise How is the garden progressing?

Philip Slowly. All this frost—and some of my best men laid up—one broke his leg and another down with a fever.

Louise You be careful—there's a lot of fever about—and you're not looking as well as usual, is he, Father?

Kendall shrugs, but does not answer. To cover the awkwardness, Louise rattles on

We saw Mary Pascoe in the village. I declare she's fatter than ever.
Father said she looked like a stuffed armchair. Wasn't it naughty of
him? Aren't you going to unwrap your gun, Philip?
Philip Of course. (*He does so*)

Seecombe enters with champagne and glasses

Louise Good afternoon, Seecombe.
Seecombe Good afternoon, Miss Louise, good afternoon, sir.

Kendall nods

Louise Oh, champagne! How lovely. We'll drink your health, Philip. I
expect all the staff drank his health yesterday, didn't they, Seecombe?
Seecombe Yes, Miss Louise.
Philip It's a beauty—thank you again.
Louise Presents are so difficult, don't you agree? What else did you get?
I know the tenants' gift—but what else?
Philip My Cousin Rachel gave me a beautiful watch.
Louise How nice—but haven't you Ambrose's?
Philip Yes.
Louise Still, I suppose it's a good thing to have two in case one goes wrong.

Seecombe hands round champagne

Oh, thank you, Seecombe.
Philip I'll have some brandy, Seecombe.

Seecombe pours brandy for Philip

Louise If I were rich I'd have champagne every night. Your health, Philip.
(*She lifts her glass and drinks*) Oh, isn't it delicious? I could go on
drinking it for ever.

The sound of a carriage is heard

Philip Excuse me . . .

Philip hurries off, his face alight

Louise It must be *her*.
Kendall Drink up, Louise, you forced me to come and I came. Now we are
going.
Louise But, Father . . .
Kendall Hurry up.
Louise Oh, very well. Yes, I realize you're furious with Philip—I think
he's crazy myself but it *was* his birthday and . . . (*She breaks off*)

Philip enters with Rachel. He is all eager but she is very composed

Rachel (*to Philip*) I had to go into Bodmin on business, Philip. I didn't
think it necessary to consult you . . . Ah, Louise—and Mr Kendall . . .

Kendall bows

Louise Oh, er—good afternoon.

Philip Champagne, Rachel?

Rachel (*coolly*) Thank you, no.

Philip Seecombe see that the carriage goes round to the stables immediately. We shall not be needing it again.

Seecombe exits

Rachel looks coolly at Kendall and Louise. Philip looks puzzled

Louise We brought Philip's present over—that's it.

Rachel How very nice—but hasn't he several already?

Louise Yes. He's very fortunate. Several guns and two watches.

Kendall (*abruptly*) We must be going. Come on, Louise . . .

Philip A moment, please. Let me refill your glasses.

Kendall No, thank you, Philip.

Philip I insist. (*He fills their glasses—he is a little drunk*) I have a very important toast. Since last night I have been the happiest of men. I believe, Uncle Nick, all our differences will be forgotten when I tell you and Louise to drink to Rachel—who is to be my wife.

A gasp from Louise

Rachel Have you quite lost your senses, Philip?

Philip I am sorry it is premature, dearest, but—they are my oldest friends.

Rachel I think his birthday and the drink have gone to Philip's head. I apologize for this schoolboy folly, I trust you will forget it.

Philip What are you saying, Rachel? You gave me your promise. You gave me your promise last night.

Rachel I think you had better go to your room, Philip, before you do any more damage.

Kendall Come, Louise.

Rachel Mr Kendall, I know for some reason you have ceased to approve of me—but I do assure you there is not a word of truth in what Philip is saying.

Kendall I'm glad to hear of it. After all there is no need for marriage, you've gained your objective without it, have you not?

Kendall goes out with Louise, leaving the door open

Rachel turns on Philip in a fury

Rachel I could kill you!

Philip But, Rachel—last night, in your bedroom—we made love.

Rachel So?

Philip You wouldn't have consented if we were not going to get married.

Rachel You fool! You stupid country-bred fool! I let you make love to me because you had given me the jewels and because I had had too much champagne—because I was fond of you—but marriage . . . My God! do you really think I'd marry a schoolboy?

Philip I can't believe it's you saying these things. Rachel—I implore you . . .

Rachel You disgust me.

Philip recoils

Philip I did not disgust you last night.

Rachel Last night never happened.

Philip Ah, but it did—when I awoke this morning you were in my arms . . .

She tries to go past him but he bars the way

Why did you go into Bodmin?

Rachel To see Mr Trewin.

Philip Was not the Deed of Gift perfectly clear?

Rachel I just wanted it verified.

Philip You haven't even thanked me.

Rachel I'd planned many things—things that would ensure you didn't suffer from giving me what was morally mine—but now—let me pass.

Philip No.

Rachel Let me pass, Philip, or I will ring for Seecombe.

Philip You whore!

She slaps his face. He staggers back, but does not allow her to pass

Rachel Let me pass.

Philip Oh, Rachel, Rachel my love, say it's all a bad dream. Say you're going to be my wife. I love you. I love you . . .

Rachel Out of my way.

There is the sound of a carriage

Who's that?

Philip I neither know nor care. Say you'll keep your promise, Rachel.

She tries to pass him, but he holds her arm. The doorbell rings

Rachel Let me go!

Philip (*quietly*) I'll never let you go, Rachel. Never. Do you understand? You're mine. After last night you're mine for ever. It is no use your trying to run away because wherever you go I will follow you. You can go to the ends of the earth and I'll be there waiting for you.

The bell rings again

You can never escape me. We are one person now and who can escape from himself? When you see your shadow you will see mine beside it. When you walk down a street, you will hear my footsteps following yours.

Rachel Philip, don't—you're frightening me.

Philip You would do well to be frightened, Rachel. You've never known love such as mine. It will be with you all your life—and mine and after your death . . .

Rainaldi, a dark good-looking man in his forties wearing a cloak and carrying a valise, enters through the open doorway

Rachel gives a little cry, frees herself and runs forward

Rachel Rainaldi! My dear, dear Rainaldi . . .

Rainaldi takes both her hands and kisses them

Rainaldi Dear Rachel ... Mr Ashley?
Philip (*shortly*) Yes.
Rachel I am so glad to see you. I did not expect you till next week.
Rainaldi My business in London was over sooner than I thought.
Rachel Oh, it is so good to see you. Where are you staying?
Rainaldi I have engaged a room at the *Rose and Crown.*
Rachel For tonight only. Tomorrow you will come here.
Rainaldi But—perhaps Signor Ashley ...
Rachel (*interrupting*) I insist. Philip, give Signor Rainaldi a glass of wine.

Dazedly, Philip pours a drink

How is my lovely Florence?
Rainaldi Very beautiful. The spring flowers are all out. The laburnums in
the sunken garden are in their full glory.
Rachel I long to see them. I am making a sunken garden here, too. I will
show you tomorrow.

Philip hands Rainaldi a glass of wine

Rainaldi Thank you, Mr Ashley. You are surprised to see me?
Philip Yes.
Rainaldi Rachel did not tell you I was in England?
Philip No.
Rainaldi I have been here three weeks. It was very cold in London.
Rachel You will find it warmer in Cornwall. How are all our friends?
Rainaldi The Paolis gave their usual Spring Ball. It was magnificent. All
Florence was there including your old admirer the Conte Firenze.
Rachel My dear Roberto—how is he?
Rainaldi As handsome as ever. Isabella was there. They say she poisoned
her husband—arsenic in the tisane.

They both laugh

Rachel And Paolo di Maggio. How is Paolo?
Rainaldi It is rumoured that he will marry the youngest Mafiola girl.
Rachel No!
Rainaldi Why not? She is young, pretty and what is more important
extremely rich.
Philip Excuse me ...

Philip goes out

Rainaldi He is not pleased. Why did you not tell him I was in England?
Rachel I was going to—why didn't you tell me you were coming today?
Rainaldi Are you not happy to see me?
Rachel I'm thankful, Rainaldi. I can't tell you how thankful.
Rainaldi Is something wrong?
Rachel Read this. (*She produces the Deed of Gift from her reticule and
hands it to him*)
Rainaldi What is it?
Rachel Read it.

Rainaldi reads the Deed

Rainaldi Rachel!

Rachel It's all mine. Everything.

Rainaldi How did you ...?

Rachel He's in love with me—the poor child.

Pause—Rachel smiles triumphantly

Rainaldi (*heavily*) Yes, the poor child.

Rachel Is it not wonderful? All our troubles are over.

Rainaldi Yes.

Rachel Why are you not pleased?

Rainaldi I cannot help being sorry for anyone who loves you, Rachel.

Rachel He'll recover. He's young.

Rainaldi There are some illnesses from which one does not recover. You are one of them.

Rachel My dear Rainaldi.

Rainaldi I should know. I have had the Rachel sickness for many years. Sometimes I think I have recovered but when I see you again I know I have not. You are under my skin, Rachel, and there is no hope for me.

Rachel I have never heard you talk like this before.

Rainaldi Nor will you again. Well—my dear, what are your plans?

Rachel I would like to leave here soon. I'm afraid all is not well between me and my cousin.

Rainaldi But he has given you everything.

Rachel Yes, but he—he imagines that I had promised to marry him.

Rainaldi And had you?

Rachel Never.

Rainaldi You sometimes give the impression, my dear, of promising things—things you have no intention of giving.

Rachel Just because I was kind to him.

Rainaldi Ah ...

Rachel I am fond of him, Rainaldi, or was. Just now he frightened me.

Rainaldi Young men take their disappointments too hard. Now, if you will accept my advice ...

Rachel I always do.

Rainaldi Well—I advise you to get on good terms with him again. It would look strange if you were not friends after his great generosity. He might make trouble.

Rachel How?

Rainaldi I am not sure that this is absolutely watertight. (*He taps the Deed of Gift*)

Rachel His lawyer says it is.

Rainaldi I would prefer an expert opinion. Till I get it, Rachel, well, you said you were fond of the boy.

Rachel I was.

Rainaldi Be fond of him again. He seems a pleasant lad—and remarkably like Ambrose.

Rachel Yes . . .

Rainaldi I must be going. The post-chaise is waiting.

Rachel I'll send the carriage round tomorrow—about eleven.

Rainaldi Are you sure it is wise?

Rachel Rainaldi—I need you.

Rainaldi When you look at me like that I am unable to resist you. (*He kisses her hands*) Until tomorrow. (*He goes to the door*) Be fond of him again, Rachel.

Rainaldi goes out

Pause. Rachel pulls the bell

Seecombe enters

Seecombe Yes, madam?

Rachel The tray, Seecombe, please. And tell Mr Philip.

Seecombe Very good, madam.

Rachel And Seecombe, we are having a visitor for a week or so. You can prepare the Blue Room—oh and see that the carriage goes to call for him at the *Rose and Crown* tomorrow at eleven.

Seecombe I saw the post-chaise, madam, as I was coming back from the stable. I hope I did not inconvenience you not being here to answer the bell.

Rachel That's all right, Seecombe. Our guest is an Italian friend of mine— a Signor Rainaldi. I will tell you about which food to order later.

Seecombe Yes, madam. Foreign Kickshaws I presume, madam?

Rachel Not at all, Seecombe—the roast beef of England.

Seecombe, looking bewildered, goes

Rachel fidgets round the room

Philip enters

Philip You wanted me?

Rachel Yes. Philip, I'm sorry. Can we not be friends?

Philip Friends?

Rachel Try to understand, my dear. I am deeply fond of you. Surely I have proved that. My affection for you led you to expect—my dear, one day, I hope it will be soon—you will meet a girl of your own age and love her. What you imagine you feel for me will be like a dream—let it not be a bad dream, Philip.

Philip It is you who do not understand, Rachel. I love you.

Rachel Philip, my dear—young men often imagine they love an older woman, but . . .

Philip (*interrupting*) Why didn't you tell me Rainaldi was in England?

Rachel I was going to tell you.

Philip Were you?

Rachel Of course. I suppose I forgot because it didn't seem very important. As to coming here—well, I was as surprised as you.

Philip I am not too pleased that you invited him to stay here in my house.

Rachel My house, Philip dear.
Philip Yes—your house.
Rachel Oh Philip, my dear, it breaks my heart to have things so wrong between us. Let us be friends. Nothing matters except that we are friends.
Philip Is that all we can be—friends?
Rachel For the moment—isn't that enough?
Philip For the moment . . .
Rachel Who knows what may happen?
Philip (*eagerly*) Rachel!

Seecombe enters with the tisane tray

Seecombe Your tisane, madam, and these came for you in the post, madam. (*He hands her a packet*)

She opens the packet

Seecombe exits

Rachel Ah—some more seeds for the garden. Coriander, Laburnum, Japonica . . .
Philip What did you mean by—"for the moment"?
Rachel It is wise not to look too far ahead.
Philip I meant what I said earlier. I will never leave you, Rachel.
Rachel Philip, that's absurd. You have your duties here. I have certain duties in Florence.
Philip Then I will accompany you.
Rachel I shall probably be accompanied by Rainaldi.
Philip That makes two of us.
Rachel Come to Florence, then, you will not like it.
Philip I shall be with you.
Rachel I shall go on to Rome.
Philip It doesn't matter where you go.
Rachel Philip—this is idiotic.
Philip I have made up my mind, Rachel.
Rachel (*slowly*) Yes—yes, I can see that you have.
Philip How long will Rainaldi be here?
Rachel As long as—we have business to discuss.
Philip I shall be interested.
Rachel Private business.
Philip You can have nothing private from me any longer, Rachel.

Pause. Rachel busies herself with the tisane tray

We could get married in Florence.
Rachel Philip—Philip are you ill? You're shivering.
Philip And go to Rome for our honeymoon.
Rachel Philip—listen. Once and for all I am not going to marry you.
Philip Yes, you are. We were made for each other, Rachel.
Rachel You're mad!
Philip I love you.

She gives a shudder and hands him his cup

How wonderful to think that every day of our lives we shall be sitting somewhere, just the two of us, drinking our tisane. We shall grow older but it will be just the same—you will always be beautiful and I shall always adore you. We won't need other people because we shall have each other. You will send Rainaldi packing . . .

Rachel No.

Philip Oh yes, my dear . . . (*He pulls a face*) This tisane is more bitter than usual.

Rachel Philip—you *are* ill.

Philip It is very warm . . .

Rachel pulls the bell

The summer will soon be here. You'll like Barton in the summer, Rachel. We'll go down to the sea—the sea . . . (*The cup falls from his hand*) And we will go out into the meadows, and make love, and the sky will be so blue, so blue . . . (*He falls back in the sofa*)

Seecombe enters

Rachel Mr Philip is ill, Seecombe.

Seecombe goes to him

Seecombe Mr Philip . . .

Philip Just the two of us. Just the two of us . . . (*He collapses on to the floor*)

The Lights fade

SCENE 3

The same. A few days later. Afternoon

The front door is open

Rainaldi is standing by the window. Rachel comes downstairs

Rainaldi How is he?

Rachel He has a very high fever.

Rainaldi What does the doctor say?

Rachel He is worried. He is afraid it is affecting the brain.

Rainaldi Like Ambrose.

Rachel Yes. Strange isn't it?

Rainaldi Very strange.

Rachel Why are you looking at me like that?

Rainaldi I was just thinking how unfortunate it was that you discovered that Ambrose had not signed the will until *after* he was dead.

Rachel What *do* you mean?

Rainaldi We were so sure he had signed it. Oh well, it doesn't matter now.

All is well. You have all that he would have left you—and more—but it would be a pity if Philip were to die—like Ambrose.

Rachel Why should he? He is young and strong.

Rainaldi Then we must hope that his youth and strength will pull him through—for his sake—and yours.

Rachel I don't understand you.

Rainaldi I think you do.

Rachel (*defensively*) He went swimming and caught a chill.

Rainaldi Yes?

Rachel It's the truth.

Rainaldi I'm sure it is.

Rachel You sound as if you didn't believe me.

Rainaldi I believe he went swimming and caught a cold.

Rachel What are you trying to say?

Rainaldi What I have said. Nurse him very carefully, Rachel.

Rachel Why do I put up with you, Rainaldi?

Rainaldi Habit, my dear. Or perhaps you cannot do without me.

Rachel I can do without you very well. I can do without any man!

Rainaldi But you cannot do without the things that you gain through men. You use us like pawns in the chess game of your life. We are expendable. But take care you do not become reckless and make a false move.

Rachel I know what I am doing.

Rainaldi Do you?

Rachel (*lightly*) I am nursing a poor boy to whom I am devoted, making a sunken garden, and looking after my property.

Their eyes meet

Rainaldi I see.

Rachel I hope you do. It would be sad if we were to misunderstand each other after all these years.

Rainaldi I shall never misunderstand you, Rachel. Love has not blinded me.

Rachel No?

Rainaldi No.

She smiles suddenly and holds out her hand. He kisses it

Rachel, why do you think I am here?

Pause. Rachel suddenly laughs

Rachel You are my friend, Rainaldi.

Rainaldi Your friend. How long is it since we first met?

Rachel I don't remember.

Rainaldi I do. Sixteen years. At the Paolis. You were nineteen. You came into the ballroom wearing yellow taffetas, and the famous yellow diamonds of the Sangaletti. I was twenty-four; and when I looked at you, it was as if the stars had come out in Heaven. (*He laughs*) What did you think of me?

Rachel I thought you looked—interesting.

Rainaldi Only interesting!

Rachel Very interesting.

Rainaldi Perhaps if I had had money and a title. These things meant a great deal—to your mother. She was a woman of great appetite. She brought you up with a wrong sense of values, my poor Rachel—you were marred in the making. But what does it matter? You are Rachel. A creature of impulse; a creature of moods, of contradictions. You can be kind, you can be cruel; lovable-spiteful, sensual-puritanical. Unforgettable. You are Rachel. And I cannot do without you any more than you can do without me. And why? Because you lead a stormy life, my dear. A ship on a rough sea needs a steady helmsman. I am he.

Louise enters hurriedly by the front door

Louise Mrs Ashley—they are saying in the village that Philip is very ill.

Rachel I'm afraid he is—Miss Kendall—Signor Rainaldi.

Rainaldi Enchanted.

Louise How do you do? (*To Rachel*) What is the matter with him?

Rachel He went swimming—you remember—and caught a chill. Now he has a fever.

Louise Can I see him?

Rachel I'm afraid not.

Louise Why not?

Rainaldi If you will excuse me—I have some business to attend to.

Rainaldi goes quickly upstairs and off

Louise Why not?

Rachel He is not well enough to see anyone at present.

Louise *You* see him.

Rachel That is different.

Louise Why is it different?

Rachel Miss Kendall, I know you are an old friend of Philip's—but . . .

Louise Oh, why did you ever come here?

Rachel I beg your pardon.

Louise You have bewitched him. He's not the Philip I knew—you *must* have promised to marry him.

Rachel I assure you I did not.

Louise Then why did he say you were going to be his wife?

Rachel He was not himself.

Louise Why?

Rachel Miss Kendall, this is a profitless discussion.

Louise He has not been himself ever since he met you. Before you came he hated you for what you had done to Ambrose.

Rachel I think you had better go before you say anything you will regret.

Louise You're an evil woman. You are notorious in Florence and you come here as mild as milk and bewitch a simple boy. You get him to give you all he possesses, and now that he is ill, I suppose you'll leave him, having squeezed him dry.

Rachel I shall ring for Seecombe to show you out.

Louise I am not going without seeing Philip.

Rachel You are not seeing him.

Louise What right have you to prevent me?

Rachel Every right. This is my house.

Louise You may own the house, but you don't own Philip.

Pause

Rachel Miss Kendall, be reasonable. Philip is ill. Too ill to see anyone. He has a bad fever. The doctor fears it may affect his brain.

Louise As it did Ambrose. Strange that Philip should suffer in the same way as his cousin.

Rachel I am ringing for Seecombe.

Louise bars her way to the bell

Louise That would be foolish. If it were known locally, and I would make sure it was known—ordering me out of the house of my oldest friend would not add to your popularity.

Rachel My popularity as you call it is a matter of supreme indifference to me.

Louise I think not. You have done everything to court it. Visited the tenants, given them presents, flattered the County, charmed the Vicar. But perhaps now that you have everything, you will give up bothering.

Rachel If you will not go—then I will leave you.

Louise I am seeing Philip.

Rachel No, Miss Kendall.

Louise I will see him.

Rachel Have you no pride, no modesty? A young girl chasing a young man the way you chase Philip is most unseemly. If you were my daughter I would be ashamed of you.

Louise Thank God I am not your daughter, for I would be ashamed of *you*.

Rachel starts to speak

Philip appears suddenly at the top of the stairs. He looks very ill and wild

Rachel Philip! Go back to bed at once!

Philip Rachel—where have you been? (*He starts to stumble down the stairs*)

Rachel Philip, my dear, go back to bed. You are ill.

Philip I was asleep and you were not there.

Rachel I'll take you back and stay with you. Come . . .

Louise Philip!

Philip She wasn't there, Louise. My wife wasn't there.

Rachel Come.

Philip I'm so thirsty.

Rachel I'll make you some tisane.

Philip It's so bitter. Why is it so bitter, Rachel?

Rachel (*to Louise*) Ring for Seecombe.

Louise does so, she is shattered

Seecombe will bring you some lemonade.

Philip A wife should stay with her husband. Why did you not stay with me, Rachel?

Rachel I'll stay with you, Philip. I'll stay with you.

Philip You were sitting beside me. The sun was in your hair.

Rachel Let us go upstairs. I promise I'll sit beside you . . .

Philip The sun was in your hair . . .

Seecombe enters

Seecombe Mr Philip!

Rachel Help me get him back to bed, Seecombe.

Seecombe Yes, madam.

Seecombe goes to Philip and between them they help him up the stairs. Louise stands rigid

Seecombe and Rachel go off with Philip

Louise sinks down on the sofa and buries her face in her hands. She begins to cry

Rainaldi enters in a travelling-cloak, carrying a valise

Louise looks up

Rainaldi Miss Kendall—you are unwell.

Louise No, no I am all right, thank you.

Rainaldi Is there anything I can do?

Louise No, there is nothing anyone can do. (*She rises*) Good-bye, Signor.

Louise goes out

Rainaldi looks after her, puzzled

Seecombe comes down the stairs

Rainaldi Oh, Seecombe . . .

Seecombe Yes, sir.

Rainaldi I presume that Mrs Ashley is looking after her patient.

Seecombe Yes, sir.

Rainaldi Give her this, will you? (*He hands him a note and picks up his valise*)

Seecombe You're not leaving, sir?

Rainaldi I'm afraid so. Guests are not welcome in a house where there is sickness.

Seecombe I will order the carriage to be sent round.

Rainaldi No need. It is but a step to the village and I can get a post-chaise. (*He hands Seecombe some money*)

Seecombe Thank you, sir.

Rainaldi Thank you for looking after me so well.

Rainaldi nods at Seecombe and goes off. Rachel appears at the head of the stairs

Rachel Mr Philip would like some lemonade, Seecombe.
Seecombe Very good, madam. The Signor left this note for you.
Rachel What do you mean?
Seecombe He's gone, madam, and left you this note.
Rachel Gone?
Seecombe Yes, madam.

Rachel comes down the stairs and takes the note

I'll fetch the lemonade, madam.

Seecombe goes off to the servants' quarters

Rachel tears open the note and reads it. She looks puzzled, reads it again then crumples it up

Seecombe enters with a jug on a tray

Rachel Seecombe, I shall want the carriage tomorrow afternoon.
Seecombe Very good, madam.
Rachel Miss Kendall?
Seecombe She must have gone while we were with Mr Philip, madam.
Rachel Yes. Thank you, Seecombe. I'll take that. (*She takes the jug from him*) I shall be sitting with Mr Philip. See that we are not disturbed.
Seecombe Very good, madam.

Rachel goes off upstairs

Seecombe stands looking after her. The Lights fade

SCENE 4

The same. Afternoon, three weeks later

Philip, better but shaky and in a dressing-gown, is being helped down the stairs by James. Seecombe enters

Seecombe That's right—slowly does it. Over to the fire, Mr Philip. You must keep warm.

James steers Philip to a chair before the fire

It's good to see you up again, sir.
Philip How long has it been, Seecombe?
Seecombe A good three weeks, sir. You had us very worried, sir, you had never been as ill in your life. (*To James*) That'll do, boy.

James goes off

Philip Where's the mistress?
Seecombe Gone shopping, sir. She goes regular like most afternoons, buying new curtains and such like. "Seecombe," she says to me, "Seecombe, you won't know the place when I've finished with it." By

the way, sir, you remember those clothes of Mr Ambrose's you gave me to give to the tenants?

Philip Of course. I hope they were appreciated.

Seecombe Oh yes, indeed, sir. I took the liberty of keeping his jacket for myself, sir.

Philip I'm glad—Mr Ambrose would have been glad too.

Seecombe I wore it for the first time yesterday and I found this in the pocket. It's addressed to you, sir. (*He hands him a letter*)

Philip From Mr Ambrose?

Seecombe Looks like he didn't have time to post it.

Philip Yes. Thank you, Seecombe.

Seecombe Can I get you anything, sir?

Philip What—oh, yes, a hot brandy and water.

Seecombe Very good, sir.

Seecombe goes out

Philip opens the letter

Philip (*reading slowly*) "Philip—they are plotting something—Rachel and Rainaldi. When I approach they fall silent. They want me out of the way. Can they be plotting to murder me? Come quickly for God's sake."

James comes in with the hot brandy and water. He puts it down by Philip, then makes a grimace of pain and puts his hand to his ear

(*dully*) What's the matter?

James It's the ear-ache, Mr Philip. I've got it cruel. 'Tis all that waiting on the quayside every afternoon for the mistress. It was that bad, William took my place today.

Philip The quayside? There are no shops on the quayside.

James No, sir, but the mistress goes to the *Rose and Crown* to see the foreign gentleman.

Philip The foreign gentleman?

James The one what was staying here. Will that be all, sir?

Philip Yes, that will be all.

James goes

Philip takes out the letter and reads it again. There is the sound of a carriage approaching. He puts the letter away and takes a sip of brandy

Rachel enters

Rachel Philip! My dear, how good to see you up again!

Philip You've been shopping.

Rachel Oh, Philip—should you be drinking brandy? Let me make you a tisane.

Philip No, thank you. What did you buy?

Rachel Oh, this and that—hangings for the Blue Room.

Philip I'd like to see them.

Rachel So you shall.

Philip Where are they?

Rachel They're sending them by carrier. How are you feeling, Philip?

Philip A bit weak. What else did you buy?

Rachel I really can't remember. Are you warm enough, my dear? It's nearly May—but very chilly out.

Philip Yes, it must be cold by the sea. There's always a wind on the quayside.

Rachel I must go and take off my things. Shall we have an early supper?

Philip Why not?

Rachel I've ordered your favourite—boiled chicken with bacon and parsley sauce.

Philip Which you never had in Italy.

Rachel No—we cook chicken in many different ways but not with bacon and parsley sauce. Personally, I find it delicious.

Philip I'm glad. I wonder if your friend Signor Rainaldi would agree. How long ago did he leave us—I forget.

Rachel Several weeks now, he felt that guests should not intrude when there is sickness in the house.

Philip How wise, so he went to the *Rose and Crown* instead?

Their eyes lock. There is a pause

Rachel (*steadily*) Yes, he went to the *Rose and Crown* instead.

Philip And you visit him every afternoon?

Rachel We have business to discuss.

Philip Why did you lie to me—saying you were shopping?

Rachel Because I know you hate Rainaldi.

Philip Yes, I hate him.

Rachel He is the only true friend I have in the world. He knows me for what I am and it makes no difference.

Philip And what are you?

Rachel A woman. A woman like all others. A creature of impulse. Someone with all the human weaknesses. Good and bad mixed together. A woman who has known great sorrow.

Philip Such as?

Rachel I loved Ambrose. He died.

Philip hands her the letter

What's this?

Philip Read it.

She does so

Rachel My poor Ambrose. My poor, poor Ambrose.

Philip Is Rainaldi your lover?

Rachel How dare you!

Philip Why did you not marry him when Ambrose died? Ah, but I was forgetting—you had not got the money then.

Rachel Philip!

Philip What a fool I've been. How you must have laughed at me.

Rachel No, Philip, no.

Philip (*taking back the letter and reading*) "Are they plotting to murder me?"

Rachel He was out of his mind.

Philip I wonder.

Rachel You are out of your mind, too, to take any notice of such a letter.

Philip I *was* out of my mind.

Rachel Philip, you are still not well. You don't know what you are saying.

Philip Ah, but I do, Rachel. I am saying that Rainaldi is your lover and that Ambrose died very conveniently.

Rachel I am leaving this house tomorrow, or you are.

Philip Where do you suggest I go?

Rachel Wherever you wish.

Philip Florence? I would like a word with Ambrose's doctor.

Rachel Why?

Philip His collapse was very sudden, was it not?

Seecombe enters with the tisane tray

Rachel Thank you, Seecombe.

Philip I'll have another hot toddy, Seecombe.

Seecombe Very good, sir.

Seecombe goes, taking the brandy glass

Philip Hot brandy may not be good for me but at least it's safe.

Rachel I am beginning to understand.

Philip Good.

Rachel You believe the letter—you think Ambrose did not die naturally?

Philip I only know what he said in this letter—and the other letters.

Rachel The other letters?

Philip Why do you think I went to Florence?

Rachel Because Ambrose was ill.

Philip Because Ambrose was ill—and frightened. Because of what he had written about you.

Rachel What did he say?

Philip He said money was the only way to your heart. He said you lied. I know you lie. He said: "She has done for me, Rachel, my torment . . ."

Rachel (*in a whisper*) He said that . . .

Philip He begged me to come quickly. I came. I found he had died suddenly and was buried just as suddenly—and now I find that—(*he taps the letter*)—Rainaldi is at the *Rose and Crown*. I have also had a fever—an unaccountable fever. I find it—strange.

Rachel Are you accusing me of murdering Ambrose?

Philip I said I found it—strange.

Rachel I am trying to keep calm, Philip. I find it difficult. I am saying to myself—he is still a sick man. But however sick you are—what you are saying is monstrous. So monstrous it is almost laughable—if I could laugh. You are accusing me and my dear Rainaldi of—of murdering Ambrose. Why? Why? I had nothing to gain by his death. He left nothing to me—I had everything to lose. A husband, a home, everything. Your insane jealousy of Rainaldi has upset the balance of your mind, Philip. What you are saying to me is actionable—if I wished to take action. But I have been fond of you—very fond and very grateful and now that you are better, I am returning to Florence.

Philip When?

Rachel The day after tomorrow.

Philip Don't go!

Rachel After such an accusation, how can I stay?

Philip I don't care what you have done. I love you.

Rachel Oh, Philip . . .

Philip I love you with every bit of my being. I *cannot* lose you. I know you lie. I know that money is your God. I know you plotted with Rainaldi—but it doesn't matter. You are my life, Rachel. Without you I am nothing. Without you I cannot go on living. Say my suspicions have been a bad dream. You loved me once—say you love me still.

Rachel I loved you? I never loved you. Not for an instant.

Philip Not—for—an—instant . . .?

Rachel A green boy like you? I have known men.

Seecombe enters with the hot toddy

Seecombe Here you are, sir.

Rachel Seecombe, I shall be leaving for Italy the day after tomorrow.

Seecombe Oh, madam—will you be gone long?

Rachel Some time, I think. I have a lot to do and many friends to see.

Seecombe We shall miss you, madam, all of us.

Rachel I should like the carriage brought round about four o'clock. I shall spend the night in Bodmin.

Seecombe Yes, madam. It's a pity you have to go before the sunken garden is quite finished.

Rachel When I return—perhaps next year—the bulbs will have had time to grow and the trees will be out.

Seecombe Next year, madam. That's a long time—isn't it, Mr Philip?

Philip Yes.

Seecombe As I said, we will miss you, madam.

Rachel Thank you, Seecombe.

Seecombe Have you finished with the tray, madam?

Rachel Yes, you may take it.

Seecombe takes the tray and goes

Philip I suppose Rainaldi will be going with you.

Rachel Yes.

Philip I expect, also, that you will want me to go on managing the estate while you are away.

Rachel Why not? What else can you do? You have no profession.

Philip No.

Rachel Oh, Philip—why do you force me to be so cruel?

Philip I force you?

Rachel Tear up Ambrose's letters. Give your jealousy and your absurd suspicions nothing to feed on. They do not harm me, Philip, they harm you.

Philip I believe Ambrose. He would not have written such letters without cause.

Rachel You've kept them from me all these months.

Philip Yes. The moment I saw you I loved you. I believed what you said about his illness changing him.

Rachel It's the truth.

Philip You never had any pearls, your first husband was killed in an accident, Rainaldi had gone back to Italy—you have lied to me so often, Rachel, why should you not lie about Ambrose's death?

Rachel You have not an atom of proof.

Philip No.

Rachel If one word of your wild accusations got to Rainaldi's ears . . .

Philip What then?

Rachel He is a lawyer. He would know what to do. (*She moves towards the stairs*)

Philip Where are you going?

Rachel To my room. To pack.

The Lights fade

SCENE 5

The same. Afternoon, two days later

Philip is sitting in the armchair staring at nothing. Seecombe enters

Seecombe Excuse me, sir, I have a message from the foreman who's working on the ravine in the sunken garden.

Philip Oh, yes?

Seecombe It's about the bridge across it, sir.

Philip Yes?

Seecombe Well, he asked me to tell you it weren't safe to stand on, sir. The supports aren't in yet, so it won't take no weight—and the drop is twenty-five feet, sir . . .

Philip Thank you, Seecombe, *I'll remember.*

James appears at the head of the stairs, carrying a trunk

Seecombe Put that in the porch, James.

James Yes, Mr Seecombe.

Seecombe Is that the lot?

James One more to come.

James goes out with the trunk

Seecombe Yes, we're going to miss Mrs Ashley, sir.

Philip does not reply. Seecombe turns to go—then, remembering something, turns back

Oh and Tamlyn says can he cut down the laburnum in the Long Walk—
they're hanging over the wall into Lacy's Meadows where the cows are,
and their seeds is poison.

Philip Poison? Laburnum seeds?

Seecombe Didn't you know that, Mr Philip, and you a country boy?
Deadly poison they are. The Tregassick boys ate them and all three of
them died. I remember the funeral—from here to Bodmin and all the
women crying.

Philip Laburnum seeds . . .

The doorbell rings

Seecombe Now who can that be? (*He goes to open the door*)

Louise and Kendall enter. Seecombe goes off to the servants' quarters

Philip (*rising*) Louise! Uncle Nick!

Kendall Louise insisted on coming and she wouldn't come alone. Besides
I wanted to see you—about business.

Philip Yes?

Kendall Later.

Louise It's wonderful to see you well and about again.

Kendall You've had a bad time, by all accounts.

Philip Yes—what can I offer you?

Kendall Nothing. I must see Tamlyn before he goes. I'll call back for
Louise and we can talk then.

James enters and goes upstairs

Philip Please have a drink before you go, Uncle Nick—to show there's no
ill-feeling.

Kendall Very well.

Philip goes and pours wine

Louise You're thinner.

Kendall What exactly was the matter?

Philip A fever. Dr Mortimer was puzzled—he said it looked like Roman
fever . . .

Louise Roman fever—here in Cornwall . . .

Philip Yes. (*Handing him a glass*) Here you are, sir. Louise?

Louise No, thank you.

Kendall We were all very worried, I don't mind telling you.

Louise You ought to go away for a holiday.

Philip I'm thinking of going abroad. It'll probably be a wild goose chase,
but there's someone I particularly want to see—a doctor.

Louise A doctor? Then you still aren't well . . .

Philip I'm not seeing him on my account.

Louise Oh?

James comes downstairs with a trunk and goes out

Kendall You're going so soon, Philip?

Philip No. Mrs Ashley is leaving this afternoon.
Louise What!
Philip Are you surprised?
Louise Yes—yes, I suppose I am.
Kendall She is returning to Florence?
Philip Yes.
Kendall Very wise of her. There has been much talk in the neighbourhood . . .

Kendall goes out

Louise Why is she going so suddenly? When I came to see you when you were ill, she said nothing about going.
Philip Did you come to see me?
Louise Yes—don't you remember?
Philip No.
Louise You came down and spoke to me.
Philip I don't remember.
Louise She said I wasn't to see you and I was angry, and then you came down looking for her.
Philip You don't like her, do you?
Louise No.
Philip Why?

James enters and goes upstairs

Louise Because of what she did to you and what she might have done to Ambrose. Thank God I came that afternoon . . .
Philip Yes.

There is a pause

Louise Phil—can I ask you something?
Philip Of course.
Louise You won't be angry?
Philip No.
Louise Promise?
Philip Promise.
Louise Did she ever say she loved you?
Philip I—I took it for granted.
Louise She was your mistress?
Philip Louise!
Louise You said you wouldn't be angry.
Philip I regarded her as my wife.
Louise It—it all happened before you had given her Barton?
Philip Yes.
Louise And afterwards?
Philip There was no afterwards.
Louise Oh, poor Philip! My dear, dear Philip . . .
Philip Don't be sorry for me, Louise. (*There is a pause*)

Louise Philip—do you—do you believe what you believed about Ambrose
—before she came here?

Before he can reply—Rachel's voice is heard off upstairs

Rachel (*off*) That is all thank you, James.
James (*off*) Very good, madam.

*Rachel appears at the head of the stairs, followed by James carrying a
parcel*

Rachel Ah, Miss Kendall. (*She descends the stairs*) How very pleasant.
(*She goes to Louise and Philip*)

James goes out

Isn't it wonderful to see Philip well again? He's quite his old self, don't
you think?
Louise Yes.
Rachel You must look after him for me while I am away.
Louise You are going for long?
Rachel Who can tell? Florence is so beautiful at this time of the year. And
so gay. We go for picnics up in the hills and take musicians with us.
They play while we eat and drink the Tuscan wine. You have not been
to Italy, Miss Kendall?
Louise No.
Rachel Ah—you should. Perhaps on your honeymoon. Italy is the only
place for honeymoons.
Louise Did you spend both yours there, Mrs Ashley?
Rachel Dear Miss Kendall, how clever of you to guess. Now, Philip, I am
going to have a last look at our sunken garden. The bridge over the
ravine is up and the garden should be ready for planting quite soon. I
have left instructions with the gardeners and they know precisely what to
do.

James comes in from outside, and goes off to the servants' quarters

The foreman is a very intelligent man. I must employ him again. I have
a fancy for a gazebo on the knoll above the lakes where the azaleas grow.
I shall not be long. Will you be here when I return, Miss Kendall?
Louise I may not be. My father is coming to collect me.
Rachel Give him my good wishes. It has been some time since he called on
me. I shall not be long, Philip. What a beautiful afternoon. I almost
wish . . .
Philip Yes?
Rachel That I was not going. I have come to love Cornwall and I have a
fancy that I shall leave part of me behind—among the wild seas and the
grey rocks, and when I am sitting in the garden of the villa, drinking my
tisane under the laburnums, I shall remember stormy skies and cobbled
streets . . . But I shall have the sunshine—and without sunshine I cannot
live. (*She smiles and turns to go*)
Philip (*urgently*) Have a care!

She turns back

Rachel Have a care?

Philip (*slowly*) Do not walk too much in the sun.

Rachel (*smiling*) I always walk in the sun, Philip—did you not know that?

Rachel unfurls her parasol and goes out slowly

Louise looks at Philip. He is evidently in a terrible state of nervous tension

Louise Philip! What's the matter? Do you mind so terribly that she is going?

Philip Louise—do you believe in justice?

Louise Justice?

Philip Do you believe in retribution?

Louise I don't know what you're talking about.

Philip When the law is powerless, has a man the right to take the law into his own hands?

Louise I still don't know what you're talking about.

Philip I loved Ambrose, Louise. He was the father I had never known. We had wonderful times together. We would go riding across the fields down to the sea and watch the fishing boats. When the catch came in, we'd go down to the quay and buy pollock and bring it back and Seecombe would take them and tell cook how to make the special pollock pie with potatoes and cheese on the top. After dinner we would sit by the fire and talk. Ambrose would tell me what Barton was like when he was a boy and his mother was alive. How they gave great balls and all the countryside came in their finery. How his mother used to wear the pearl collar—the pearl collar . . .

Louise Philip, you're ill.

Philip (*hysterically*) Vengeance is mine, I will repay, said the Lord. But He doesn't, Louise. He doesn't.

Louise Sit down and rest and I . . .

Philip (*interrupting*) Rest? You tell me to rest? I don't think I'll ever rest again, Louise. You see, I'll never be really sure. I *must* be sure. I *am* sure.

Louise Sure of what?

Philip It all adds up, the letters, his death, the lies, the laburnum seeds, Rainaldi—yes, it all adds up. But there is no proof—there never will be any proof. I had to do it, Louise—I had to do it . . . (*Abruptly*) Remember Hamlet . . .?

Louise Hamlet? I read him at school but I don't see . . .

Philip (*interrupting*) Hamlet had no proof either, or he would have acted sooner . . . What was that? Did you hear anything?

Louise No.

Philip Ambrose loved life. He was still a young man, Louise, in his forties. He'd looked forward to seeing the trees he had planted grow tall and strong. The larch plantation, Louise—he told me, "As your sons grow tall, so will the larches, Philip . . ." (*He sinks down and buries his face in his hands*)

Louise Philip . . .

Philip I've been through Heaven and Hell—I am in Hell now, Rachel, my torment . . .

Louise You've the fever again, Philip. Now please . . .

Philip (*interrupting*) Ambrose took me once to the cross-roads to see a man they had hanged for murdering his wife. They used to hang murderers at the cross-roads you know. He was swinging there in the wind like a sack, his face shrunk like leather, his hands . . . (*He buries his face in his hands*)

Louise (*interrupting*) Stop Philip! It's horrible! Stop!

Kendall enters. He looks at Philip, then turns to Louise

Kendall Anything wrong?

Louise Philip—he's—he's still not quite well.

Kendall Then I'll be brief.

Louise makes a movement

If you'll just wait in the porch a moment, my dear.

Louise goes out, with a worried backward look at Philip

I've had a letter from Couch.

Philip looks up

Are you sure you're all right?

Philip nods

He says Mrs Ashley has been to see him. She's given back the jewels.

Philip (*dully*) She's what?

Kendall (*patiently*) Given back the jewels and revoked the Deed of Gift. She said she'd come to the conclusion that it was grossly unfair and that anyway she preferred to live in Italy. We've misjudged her Philip.

Philip jumps to his feet—horrified

I am very much to blame. That friend of Louise's—I've learned that her mother is well-known for spreading scandal. What is it? Philip you're shaking!

Philip Nothing—nothing.

Kendall Couch asked her why she had accepted everything in the first place, and she said she had taken them because it was so incredibly immature of you to give everything away to a woman you hardly knew, and she was afraid you were not a responsible person to leave in charge of Ambrose's beloved Barton. I've come to the conclusion that she really loved Ambrose, Philip.

Philip Oh, my God!

Suddenly there are a series of screams off

Kendall Louise!

Kendall runs out

Philip (*gabbling*) I had to do it—I didn't know—I had to do it—oh, God, I didn't know . . . (*He sinks to his knees on the floor*)

Kendall enters, half-carrying an hysterical Louise

Louise The bridge—she stood on it—she stood on it—she fell—Father, she fell . . .

Kendall drops her into a chair

Kendall Who fell?
Louise Mrs Ashley.

Kendall stares at Louise for a second and then runs out

Philip—she fell . . .

Philip, by now totally unhinged by what he has done, looks at her quite calmly

Philip (*quietly*) They used to hang murderers at the cross-roads but not any more. There they used to swing in the wind—to and fro, to and fro, to and fro, to and fro, to and . . .

The CURTAIN *slowly falls*

FURNITURE AND PROPERTY LIST

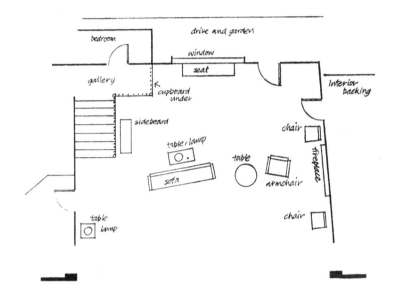

ACT I

SCENE 1

On stage: Sofa. *On it:* cushions
Armchair. *On it:* cushions
2 upright chairs
Window-seat
Lamp table above sofa
Circular table beside armchair
Lamp table below stairs
Sideboard. *On it:* 2 candles in candlesticks, matches, lamp, dressing.
  In cupboards: brandy, wine, various glasses, corkscrew
Other furniture as desired for dressing
Fender (down C)
Log fire grate
Fire-irons
On wall above sideboard: bell-push

Off stage: *Off stage:* Lit candle in jam-pot (**Seecombe**)
Valise (**James**)
Travelling-case (**Philip**)

SCENE 2

Off stage: Leather case (**Kendall**)

Personal: **Kendall:** armband, spectacles
               Philip: wrapped necklace, 2 letters
               Louise: riding-crop

SCENE 3

Set: Flowers and silver bowl on table

Off stage: Lighted candle in candlestick (**Rachel**)
               Tisane tray—i.e. silver tray with teapot, hot water jug, cups, saucers (**Seecombe**)

SCENE 4

Strike: Tisane tray

Set: **Rachel's** shawl on window-seat
               Candle and stick back on sideboard
Off stage: Silver dish with ratafia biscuits (**Seecombe**)
               Tray with decanters of port, sherry, madeira (**James**)
               2 large trunks. *In one:* books; *in the other:* Jacket, old hat, clothing as dressing (**Seecombe, James**)
               Tisane tray (**Seecombe**)

SCENE 5

Strike: Plate of biscuits
               Dirty glasses
               Trunk and contents

Off stage: Document (**Kendall**)
               Tisane tray (**Seecombe**)
               Salver with several letters (**Seecombe**)

SCENE 6

Set: Christmas tree in tub below stairs
               2 mirrors on walls

Off stage: List and pile of cards (**Seecombe**)
               2 parcels (**Louise**)
               Apron for **Rachel** (**Seecombe**)

Personal: **Philip:** pearl collar
               Rachel: box containing cuff-links
               Kendall: handkerchief

ACT II
SCENE 1

Strike: Christmas tree
                 Dirty glasses

Set: Fresh drinks and glasses in sideboard

Off stage: Tray with bottle of champagne and 2 glasses (**Seecombe**)
                 Portrait of Seecombe (**Seecombe**)
                 Large wicker hamper containing jewellery (**Seecombe**)

Personal: **Philip:** document

SCENE 2

Strike: Dirty glasses
                 Champagne
                 Hamper and jewels

Set: Candlestick back on sideboard

Off stage: Parcel containing gun (**Louise**)
                 Tray of champagne and 3 glasses (Seecombe)
                 Valise (**Rainaldi**)
                 Tisane tray (**Seecombe**)
                 Small packet (**Seecombe**)

Personal: **Rachel:** reticule containing Deed of Gift

SCENE 3

Strike: Champagne
                 Dirty glasses
                 Tisane tray

Off stage: Valise, travelling cloak (**Rainaldi**)
                 Jug of lemonade on tray (**Seecombe**)

Personal: **Rainaldi:** note

SCENE 4

Off stage: Letter (**Seecombe**)
                 Glass of hot brandy and water on tray (**James**)
                 Refill for hot brandy (**Seecombe**)
                 Tisane tray (**Seecombe**)

SCENE 5

Strike: Brandy glass

Off stage: 2 trunks (**James**)   .
                 Parcel (**James**)
                 Parasol (**Rachel**)

LIGHTING PLOT

Property fittings required: 3 'oil' lamps, log fire effect in floats
Interior. A Hall. The same scene throughout

ACT I

To open: Very faint light through window. Fire out

Cue 1	**Seecombe** enters with candle *Dim spot to cover candle*	(Page 1)
Cue 2	**Philip** exits *Fade to Black-out; then up to sunny morning for Scene 2*	(Page 2)
Cue 3	**Philip:** "Mrs Ashley . . . coming here . . ." *Fade to Black-out; then up to evening light for Scene 3.* *Lamps lit*	(Page 7)
Cue 4	**Rachel** exits *Fade to Black-out; then up to sunny evening light for Scene 4.* *Fire lit*	(Page 11)
Cue 5	**Philip** runs downstairs *Fade to Black-out; then up to afternoon light for Scene 5*	(Page 22)
Cue 6	**Philip:** "Uncle Nick . . ." *Fade to Black-out; then up to winter afternoon light for* *Scene 6*	(Page 27)
Cue 7	**Rachel** and **Philip** exit *Fade to Black-out*	(Page 33)

ACT II

To open: Late evening lighting, approaching dusk. Lamp behind
sofa lit. Fire on

Cue 8	**Philip** enters *Start slow fade to dark outside*	(Page 34)
Cue 9	**Philip** turns out lamp *Fade to dark except for candle*	(Page 41)
Cue 10	**Philip** exits to **Rachel**'s room *Fade to Black-out, then up to afternoon lighting for Scene 2*	(Page 41)
Cue 11	**Philip** collapses on floor *Fade to Black-out; then up to afternoon lighting for Scene 3*	(Page 50)
Cue 12	**Rachel** goes upstairs *Fade to Black-out; then up to afternoon lighting for Scene 4*	(Page 55)
Cue 13	**Rachel:** "To my room. To pack." *Fade to Black-out; then up to afternoon lighting for Scene 5*	(Page 60)

EFFECTS PLOT

ACT I

Cue 1	As CURTAIN rises *Distant rumble of thunder*	(Page 1)
Cue 2	**James** exits through main door *Horse neighs*	(Page 1)
Cue 3	**Philip** exits *Distant rumble of thunder, sound of wind rising*	(Page 2)
Cue 4	At start of SCENE 2 *Doorbell rings twice*	(Page 2)
Cue 5	**Seecombe:** "May I remove the tray, sir?" **Philip:** "Yes." *Doorbell rings*	(Page 20)
Cue 6	At start of SCENE 5 *Doorbell rings*	(Page 22)
Cue 7	**Rachel:** "I shall not let these die." *Sound of carriage drawing up*	(Page 29)
Cue 8	**Kendall:** "My handkerchief will do." *Bell sounds*	(Page 33)
Cue 9	**Rachel:** ". . . and I'm very grateful." *Bell sounds*	(Page 33)

ACT II

Cue 10	**Philip** drinks second brandy *Sound of carriage drawing up*	(Page 42)
Cue 11	**Louise:** ". . . drinking it for ever." *Sound of carriage drawing up*	(Page 43)
Cue 12	**Rachel:** "Out of my way." *Sound of carriage drawing up*	(Page 45)
Cue 13	**Philip** holds **Rachel's** arm *Doorbell rings*	(Page 45)
Cue 14	**Philip:** ". . . there waiting for you." *Doorbell rings*	(Page 45)
Cue 15	**James** exits. **Philip** reads letter *Sound of carriage drawing up*	(Page 56)
Cue 16	**Philip:** "Laburnum seeds." *Doorbell rings*	(Page 61)